Angela Smyth is a medical journalist and author who has written extensively for health and science magazines, the women's press and national newspapers in Britain and the USA. She was Feature Writer and Deputy Editor for *Here's Health* magazine, where she covered alternative and orthodox medicine and environmental issues. She is the author of *Gentle Medicine*.

Professor Chris Thompson is a leading researcher of the causes, effects and treatment of SAD. He is Consultant Psychiatrist at the Royal South Hants Hospital, where he runs the SAD clinic. His research has been published widely in international journals and books. He is co-editor of *Seasonal Affective Disorders*, published by Clinical Neuroscience Publishers.

SAD

who gets it

•

what causes it

•

how to treat it

ANGELA SMYTH

**in consultation with
Professor Chris Thompson**

Thorsons
An Imprint of HarperCollins*Publishers*

Thorsons
An Imprint of HarperCollins*Publishers*
77–85 Fulham Palace Road,
Hammersmith, London W6 8JB

Published by Thorsons 1991
First published by Unwin Hyman Limited 1990
This edition 1995

3 5 7 9 10 8 6 4

© Angela Smyth 1990

Angela Smyth asserts the moral right to
be identified as the author of this work

A catalogue record for this book
is available from the British Library

ISBN 0 7225 2569 9

Printed in Great Britain by
HarperCollinsManufacturing Glasgow

Contents

To my parents

Acknowledgements

My thanks go to Anna Achilleos, who first introduced me to SAD and has taught me much about health and life. I am also grateful to Jennifer Eastwood, who, while battling against SAD, provided invaluable first-hand information and contacts. Thanks also go to Christopher Thompson at the University of Southampton for his medical expertise and rigorous editing and to Michael Terman at Columbia University for help and support. This book would not have been possible without the efforts of researchers all over the world, whose work has led to new discoveries of how and why SAD can be treated. Finally, I cannot thank enough all those who courageously shared with me their personal sufferings and experiences of SAD, and provided valuable case histories for this book.

'Definitions of Cognitive Distortions' and Table 3-1 from *Feeling Good* by David D. Burns, M.D., copyright © 1980 David D. Burns, M.D., by permission of William Morrow & Co. Inc., New York.

Preface

Since the early 1980s there has been a great interest in the discovery that a proportion of people suffer badly with depression in the winter. This discovery is rightly credited to workers at the National Institute of Mental Health in Washington, but the general phenomenon of seasonal changes in mood has been known for centuries. What was new and exciting about the research in Washington was the identification of a group of people who suffered very extreme winter depression and the discovery that these people responded very well to bright artificial light. This suggested that the illness might be caused by a lack of light. The syndrome does not just show itself by a depressed mood in winter. Along with it comes a range of fairly specific changes in appetite, food preference, weight and sleep which, together with the very regular seasonal change, make up a readily identifiable illness.

Are such people very rare? The answer, as you will read in the book, is no, they are not. An estimate of the proportion of adults affected in Maryland USA is about 5% – and there is another less well defined but much bigger figure for the proportion of people affected to some degree but not severely enough to be called clinically depressed.

In the years that I have been involved in treating and researching this condition I have been impressed by the havoc which regular mood swings cause in people's family, in their leisure activities and in their work. And yet they are people who, for the most part, cope well with all sorts of stresses – as long as they do not happen in winter. Even in winter, once they have recognized and have an explanation for the problems – and even more important, know how to alleviate them – they cope with considerable fortitude.

Here then we have a newly recognized illness – one which affects a lot of people to a greater or lesser extent and which now can be treated simply and effectively. Angela Smyth's book has therefore arrived at a good time to help many people cope better with winter. It describes clearly what the many symptoms of SAD are like and what we know about how they are caused. It provides sensible self-help advice not just on how to acquire and use equipment which gives artificial light, but also on how to cope with the individual symptoms of SAD, such as carbohydrate craving and sleepiness. Many of her hints and techniques will therefore be useful to people who may not have SAD but who have some of the symptoms perhaps for other reasons.

Finally, I would like to take this opportunity to express my thanks to the sufferers who I know have helped in the preparation of the book by providing case histories and examples, many of whom have also helped advance our understanding of SAD by offering themselves as subjects of research studies. In particular our thanks go to Jennifer Eastwood who set up the self-help organization, the Seasonal Affective Disorder Association (SADA) and who has done much to bring the disorder to the attention of the professional and lay public.

Christopher Thompson
Professor of Psychiatry, Southampton University

Foreword

Few people can imagine the misery of an annually recurring depressive illness which dulls and even incapacitates mind, body and spirit for four to eight months of the year. Worse still for some SAD sufferers can be the awakening in spring to a brief respite from depression, darkened by the awareness that, as the autumn leaves change colour, they will slide once more into depression and lethargy. Life will scarcely be worth living until perhaps the daffodils bloom in spring or the roses in May or June.

Imagine living with the knowledge that this misery will have to be endured for the rest of your life, that the pleasures, relationships, successes you build up during the summer will fade into obscurity as the short dark days of winter plunge you once more into a prison of darkness. And that the only way out of that prison is to kill yourself, unless you are fortunate enough to die from natural causes, an escape often longed for during the profoundest suffering of SAD.

For up to 10% of the population, winter is a time of slowing down of mind and body and loss of interest in life's normal pleasures, a time of experiencing the 'winter blues'. For a smaller number, probably only tens of thousands, SAD is Seasonal Affective Disorder, a crippling mental illness which ruins careers and relationships and brings intense suffering not only to the sufferer, but to his or her family, friends and colleagues.

An additional burden for the SAD sufferer to bear is the

stigma of mental illness. Despite the fact that many distinguished people in our society have suffered from mental illness, it is still not acceptable in some walks of life to have experience of psychiatric illness and treatment. Many people fear 'madness', both enduring it and witnessing it, and some doctors still shy away from depressed and mentally ill patients, treating them inadequately or passing them on to another health professional rather than admit their own fear, ignorance or prejudice.

Employers are often reluctant to employ staff who have a history of mental illness; what hope is there for someone who confesses to an annually recurring depressive illness which slows down his ability to think and function and allows him to perform only simple routine tasks during the winter months. Statistics have shown that it is easier to obtain a job after being in prison than with a record of mental illness. This stigma is ridiculous as the majority of people with SAD are high achievers from all walks of life including lawyers, professors, doctors, teachers, creative artists and businessmen and women. Many of them manage to hold down successful careers despite their secret suffering every winter, only revealing their misery to close family or friends or their doctor. Others gradually lose grip on their work and leisure skills as the years of illness take their toll, and they have to learn to come to terms with failure in a society where success is highly regarded and rewarded.

SAD is not a new illness; cases have been documented throughout the history of medicine and psychiatry. It is only in the last fifteen years that it has been 'rediscovered' and amazing strides have been made in its diagnosis and treatment. Many people are now able to lead normal, satisfying lives thanks to the last decade's research by a handful of dedicated doctors. Others find their symptoms alleviated to a considerable degree even if the devastation of SAD has prevented them regaining the peace of mind that so many people take for granted.

This book, a pioneer in its field, has a vital role to play in alleviating the suffering of SAD. Firstly, it will help all those who have, or think they have, SAD to discover what they can do to obtain relief from their symptoms. It will enable 'the worried well' to realize that their winter discomfort is small in comparison with others and can help them to alter their approach to life. It will tell workers in the medical and caring professions what they need to know about SAD and how they can recognize and treat it. Finally, it will alert the reader previously unaware of SAD to the devastation suffered by tens of thousands of people and their families as a result of this illness.

At least one in four of us suffers from mental illness at some time in our lives and not one of us can afford to be complacent about it. SAD, as with other forms of disease, is not something which happens to other people. It can start at any age from four to eighty-four and it can happen to you or one of your family or friends. Buy, read and digest this book; it could mean the difference between life and existence to you one day. If you are one of the fortunate people who never has to endure a depressive illness, let this book increase your awareness and tolerance of those who suffer and help to create a less hostile world for us to live in.

Jennifer Eastwood
SAD Association

Introduction

Are you aware of a change coming over you as the winter months approach? Does your energy level drop? Do you feel cold and long to stay indoors, preferably tucked under warm bedclothes or huddled beside a cosy fire?

Do your eating habits change? All summer long you were satisfied with light salads and proteins. But now do you suddenly get an insatiable desire to fill up on pasta, rice or potatoes, and even start to binge on chocolate, bread and jam or biscuits? And what about your weight? Despite every attempt to control your appetite do the pounds still pile on over the winter months?

In the dark mornings do you dread the thought of getting out of bed and dragging yourself to work? As the evenings draw in do you feel less tempted to socialize and more inclined to snooze in front of the television, avoiding all possible contact with even your nearest and dearest? Do you notice a decline in your ability to carry out even the simplest task: does housework become an unbearable chore, the slightest concentration at work an impossible feat?

Most of all, do you lose interest in life? Do you find that friends, lovers and family bring no pleasure, and that achievements and entertainment are of little significance? Is your mood shrouded in a heavy, black cloud of depression in which life has no meaning?

How do you react to spring? When the days start to lengthen and the buds show their shoots does your mood lift? Do you shed pounds within the first week and set to work with enthusiasm, making up for the time lost during the winter?

If your answer is 'yes' to most of these questions, it is likely that you are suffering from a medically recognized illness which occurs only in winter. Doctors call it seasonal affective disorder, or SAD for short. The name is very appropriate, for sadness is one of the principal symptoms of this illness, and manifests itself in varying degrees of depression and fatigue over the winter months. For some people SAD is a mild case of the winter blues which makes them feel sluggish and irritable during the winter months. In more extreme cases the illness makes it impossible to carry on a normal life: careers are ruined and relationships destroyed. Some sufferers even resort to suicide.

SAD is not a new illness. For centuries doctors have been aware of the change in mood and energy level which comes over their patients during the winter months. They used to attribute this to the drop in temperature or the effects of being cooped up indoors for long periods. In America 'cabin fever' is still a common name for the depression and fatigue experienced in northern states during the hard, bitter winters. In Norway, where in some areas the sun never shines for part of the winter, the season is referred to as 'morketiden'. This literally means 'murky times', a reference not just to the weather, but also to the mood experienced by the inhabitants.

It is only in the last fifteen years that doctors have looked more closely at the symptoms and causes of this winter syndrome, now commonly known as SAD. Through their observations of sufferers in many countries of the world they have come to the conclusion that the low energy levels, the changes in appetite, the depression, the inertia and the introversion that many of us experience in winter are due not to low temperatures and bad weather, but to lack of sunlight.

SAD has been identified in most countries of the world where the winter brings short daylight hours and long dark evenings. These are countries situated far from the equator in both northern and southern hemispheres. Short days, low temperatures and an indoor lifestyle mean inhabitants of such countries obtain very little natural daylight once winter sets in.

The discovery that lack of light is the cause of SAD has led to the development of an ingenious treatment which is presently being used to help sufferers all over the world. It consists of replacing the shortened hours of daylight with artificial light specially designed to mimic sunlight. Over the last ten years, doctors have found that regular doses of bright light can alleviate symptoms of SAD. Sufferers treated with light lose weight and become energetic, motivated and sociable. In other words, they are able to live the joyful life they know in the spring and summer while it is still the middle of winter.

Light treatment, otherwise known as phototherapy, has been used with much success in psychiatric hospitals and clinics in Northern Europe, Scandinavia, North America, Canada, Australia, the Soviet Union and Japan. Extensive research in these countries has estimated that five to ten per cent of the population suffers from severe SAD symptoms, while around twenty-five per cent experience a milder, but still problematic form of the illness. In both cases phototherapy brings a startling recovery rate: seventy-five to eighty per cent of sufferers find relief after only four days of treatment. As a result of this success with phototherapy, doctors are now encouraging SAD sufferers to buy their own equipment for self-treatment. Today, many people are discovering the benefits of phototherapy, and are successfully treating themselves for SAD and the winter blues in the comfort of their own homes.

This book traces the discovery of SAD and describes what

doctors have learned about it in more than ten years of research. Part One examines the illness in detail, looking at who suffer from SAD, where they are located and how they suffer. The chapters in this section outline the medical research which has been carried out in many countries of the world and its attempts to explain why people get SAD and how phototherapy alleviates the symptoms. Part One also investigates the link between the hibernation of animals, the winter behaviour of primitive man, and the symptoms of SAD manifested today. The final chapters of this section question the extent to which the artificial lighting in our homes and workplaces is responsible for our mood and general health.

Part Two gives an explicit description of the major symptoms of SAD. It conveys how and when the symptoms occur, using as examples case histories of SAD sufferers who have undergone treatment. The aim of this section is to provide a thorough understanding of what it feels like to have SAD, and a comprehension of some of the biological mechanisms which give rise to the symptoms.

Part Three is a complete self-help SAD programme which offers you the opportunity to establish whether you suffer from SAD and, if you do, how to go about treating it. A detailed questionnaire will help you to carry out a self-diagnosis, the results of which indicate if you will benefit from treatment. The programme then goes on to tell you how to go about getting the phototherapy treatment, how to buy safe and efficient equipment and how to get the most out of it. Then, chapter by chapter, the programme outlines how to attack the different symptoms of SAD. It offers exercises to combat negative thinking and relieve depression; it suggests a winter eating programme which will give your body the food it needs to improve your mood and nourish you through the winter without weight gain. It will help you improve the quality of your sleep, so that with fewer hours you have more energy to complete the day, without the constant fear of wintertime drowsiness. It outlines how to make the most of natural daylight both through outdoor exercise and through simple inexpensive adaptations to your indoor environment.

Depression, sleep and eating disorders have always been among the most difficult ailments for doctors to diagnose and treat. There are a few cures on offer which do not involve unpleasant, and sometimes dangerous side-effects. For many years SAD sufferers have been misdiagnosed and mistreated. Now, thanks to the research which has identified SAD as an illness and discovered an effective means of treatment, the syndrome can be recognized and successfully treated in complete safety. Thousands of sufferers have already been treated in hospitals and clinics in many countries of the world. Armed with the self-help programme outlined in this book, you too have the possibility of successful treatment if you are a SAD sufferer. You need never experience the debilitating and depressing symptoms of winter again.

SAD
Winter
Depression

PART
1

1

What is SAD?

For many centuries doctors have recognized an association between sickness and the seasons. As early as the fifth century BC, Hippocrates wrote of diseases specific to the winter, claiming doctors should take account of the seasons when prescribing treatment:

> Such diseases as increase in the winter ought to cease in the summer ... The physician too must treat disease with the conviction that each of them is powerful in the body according to the season which is most conformable to it.
> *(Hippocrates (1923-1931) Works of Hippocrates, W.H.S. Jones and E.T. Withington, eds. and trans., Harvard University Press, Cambridge, MA.)*

The early doctors were aware of the effect winter had on their patients' mood. Medical records throughout history show an increase in the incidence of 'melancholia', or depression during the winter months. But despite this early awareness, it is only in the last ten years that modern medicine has given a name and drawn up a specific list of symptoms for what has always been known casually as the 'winter blues'. Today Seasonal Affective Disorder, or SAD, is the clinical name for winter depression. Seasonal, because the ailment is influenced by the seasons, affective, because it is an expression of mood, and disorder, because in all cases it brings about a change or imbalance in the body's normal way of functioning.

WHAT ARE THE SYMPTOMS OF SAD?

SAD can be distinguished from any other illness because its symptoms are only present on a seasonal basis. SAD symptoms always start in the autumn or early winter. In countries with daylight saving their onset may be triggered by the sudden changing of the clocks, which emphasises the transition from summer to winter. The illness generally lasts for between five to seven months until spring, when the days grow significantly longer, and the symptoms disappear, leaving the sufferer perfectly healthy until the following autumn.

There are four classic symptoms experienced every autumn and winter by most SAD sufferers. Most people feel them more severely in the afternoon and evening. They are:

- increased desire to sleep
- extreme lethargy
- depression
- increased appetite which often leads to weight gain

These basic symptoms can affect people in a number of different ways. The need to sleep more can mean falling asleep early in the evening or waking later in the morning, with difficulty getting out of bed. For some SAD sufferers it can mean a constant drowsiness throughout the day. It may be a combination of all these symptoms, which results in a continuous desire to sleep.

People with SAD find they do less in the winter. But despite this decrease in activity, they still feel tired. They want to sleep more, but often find their sleep is restless and unrefreshing. The overall lack of energy leads to other problems: an inability to concentrate at work, a lack of vitality and little motivation to carry on a normal life.

Most SAD sufferers put on weight in the winter. The average gain is 9lbs (4kg), though it can be as much as 30lbs

(13kg). Eating is often a way of compensating for lack of energy. Some SAD sufferers look for foods which are high in protein, others crave carbohydrates. For many, food provides security; hence they tend to stock up and binge, rather like an animal preparing for hibernation. Some sufferers say food offers comfort and distraction when they are feeling depressed. Many patients who are normally slim and moderate eaters during the summer are alarmed to find themselves suddenly eating slice after slice of bread or devouring a whole tin of salmon or an entire packet of biscuits in one go. They feel they have lost all self-control.

Fatigue, lack of energy and the tendency to eat more all contribute to depression, a major symptom of SAD. Feelings of misery, guilt and loss of self-esteem are common, leading to hopelessness and despair. Some SAD sufferers find it impossible to work during the winter; they take time off sick or even give up their jobs. Household chores are left undone, children's school work deteriorates.

The symptoms mentioned so far are the classic signs of SAD. However, a number of other symptoms are sometimes encountered. These are the symptoms experienced by some, but not all sufferers:

- Anxiety: tension, inability to tolerate stress, phobias.
- Social problems: irritability, loss of pleasure in being with others and a desire to avoid contact, which could even turn to unwillingness to leave the home or bed.
- Loss of libido: decreased interest in sex.
- Sleep problems: although there is a tendency to sleep for longer periods, the sleep is less satisfying and more awakenings may be experienced during the night.
- Mood swings: in the spring when SAD lifts, some sufferers experience a dramatic swing in mood and a short period of hypomania, a sudden surge of energy and enthusiasm which brings problems of its own.

- Menstrual difficulties: during the winter premenstrual tension may be worse than in other seasons, bringing irritability, sleep problems, appetite changes and low energy levels.
- Hopelessness: feelings of desperation and hopelessness, which sometimes lead to over-dependence on relationships, work, home.
- Comfort eating and drinking: carbohydrate foods, alcohol, coffee.
- Increased sensitivity to pain: headaches, muscle and joint pain.
- Other physical ailments: constipation, diarrhoea, palpitations.

Every SAD sufferer has a different story to tell, for example

ELSIE:

I get very tired and lethargic and because I have no energy, all I want to do is sleep, yet when I go to bed I can't sleep. During the day the lack of energy makes me crave food, whatever I can get my hands on. Sometimes I buy a packet of iced buns and work my way through them one after the other. I usually put on about 15lbs (6.5kg) in the winter, but lose it rapidly in the spring.

I can't think straight, my mind won't work and I know I should be able to do things that I just can't do. That's where the depression comes in. You feel frustrated and depressed because you feel inadequate; you feel you're inferior and that's when you get really desperate.

For as long as I can remember, people called me lazy – my mother, my husband, my mother-in-law. I actually grew to believe I was just lazy, but then spring would come, and bingo, I'd be up in the stars; then I could do the work of two people.

JENNIFER

Around the age of 28 I noticed that my work became a tremendous burden during the winter. I had a demanding job in the music business, which gave me a lot of satisfaction the rest of the year. However, as the pressure built up that winter I finally got to the point where I felt I could no longer cope.

I knew that something was wrong, but I was not able to identify what it was. My doctor said I was overworking, and prescribed a holiday and anti-depressants. I gave up a lot of the more demanding aspects of my job, such as public speaking and radio interviews, and concentrated on easy clerical tasks. I put on weight, at first without realising it. Despite having a patient and loving husband and many loyal friends, my life became increasingly meaningless. My doctor could not tell whether I was clinically depressed or just continually miserable and finally made a diagnosis of manic depression.

Somehow I managed to get through the next three miserable months like a zombie. Then one day at the beginning of spring I sat up in bed feeling absolutely wonderful. Within a week I had lost 9lbs (4kg). That summer I worked like a fiend, trying to compensate for the winter. I also learnt to drive and started an evening course. The following autumn everything started to fall apart again. My work went downhill, I had to give up the evening class. I was constantly on anti-depressants and tranquillisers; like a walking pharmacy. Finally, I was asked to leave my job. It was the last straw, I felt that if this was what winter was going to be like for the rest of my days, then life wasn't worth living.

JONATHAN:

Each autumn, around about when the clocks change I become increasingly down in the dumps. I lose interest in everything except my bed and sleep, life just grinds to a halt. I can't get to work on time, I can't be bothered to go out or even speak to anyone on the phone. My friends don't interest me and even my girlfriend gets fed up with my black moods and irritability. During the winter I just manage to cope with work, but tend to take a lot of days off sick. Most evenings are spent alone in front of the television with a few cans of beer; drinking seems to be the only way to blot out the awful feeling that nothing is worth living for.

All of these patients were long term SAD sufferers. Several of them were misdiagnosed and consequently mistreated for many years. One of the difficulties of diagnosing SAD is that its symptoms resemble those of a number of other illnesses: there are many different types of depression, many different eating disorders and, as every doctor will tell you, fatigue is one of the most common complaints heard in the surgery.

The many similarities between the symptoms of SAD and those of other illnesses, lead to frequent incorrect diagnosis of SAD sufferers. Consequently they are deprived of an effective treatment which could relieve their symptoms and allow them to lead a normal life.

These are some of the illnesses which could be confused with SAD:

Classical Depression

Although SAD sufferers become depressed, their symptoms and the onset of their illness are different from those found in classical depression. SAD sufferers tend to eat more in the winter months, especially carbohydrates. They may also turn to stimulants such as coffee, alcohol or chocolate. Most classical depressives lose interest in food altogether. Depressives also differ from SAD patients in their sleeping habits. Most suffer insomnia: that is, they cannot sleep or they have a tendency to wake early in the morning. In contrast SAD patients experience hypersomnia (they sleep more), feel drowsy, and experience difficulty waking.

The major difference between SAD and classical depression is the fact that the onset of SAD occurs on a regular basis during the autumn and winter months, and the syndrome is relieved in the spring. Classical depression can hit at any time, it does not generally recur on a seasonal basis and is not relieved by the onset of spring. Moreover, the incidence and severity of SAD seems to be influenced by location and daylight hours. The syndrome can become worse if the sufferer moves to an area further away from the equator, where winter brings shortened daylight hours. Alternatively SAD symptoms can be relieved by a move to an area nearer to the equator. Classical depression is not influenced by location or the number of daylight hours.

The following chart outlines the major differences between SAD and classical depression.

SAD	CLASSICAL DEPRESSION
onset in autumn, relief in summer with a recurrence each year	no seasonal pattern
tendency to sleep more	difficulty in sleeping
tendency to eat more	loss of appetite
increase in weight	loss of weight/weight remains the same
mood is influenced by changes in latitude and/or hours of daylight	mood not influenced by changes in latitude or hours of daylight

The chart can be useful in distinguishing those who present typical symptoms of SAD from those suffering from classical depression. But in many cases the symptoms of SAD are not as clear-cut as those presented above, and may overlap with those of other psychiatric illnesses. Some patients have been known to suffer all the classic symptoms of SAD except the seasonal pattern, that is, they suffer SAD symptoms all year round, not just in the winter. Others may suffer five years of SAD and then develop a continuous, non-seasonal variety of depression. Some manic depressives show classic depression symptoms with a seasonal pattern. A very small number of patients have been observed who suffer from SAD in the summer not the winter. All these factors make diagnosis very difficult, and emphasise the need for stringent self-observation before jumping to a conclusion.

Low Blood Sugar

Low blood sugar, also known as hypoglycaemia, is a condition which often leaves people feeling tired and lethargic. They experience slumps in energy, especially several hours after a meal. To compensate, people with this condition crave sugary food which gives them a short energy boost before the next slump.

Underactive Thyroid

Also known as hypothyroidism, an underactive thyroid leads to a reduction in the efficiency of the thyroid gland to produce hormones which stimulate many of the body's functions. The result is a gradual slowing down of activity leading to weakness, lethargy and a tendency to gain weight easily. Inability to tolerate the cold is also a common symptom.

Anaemia

Anaemia is related to a deficiency in the blood's ability to transport oxygen. Symptoms are fatigue, intolerance to cold and a pale skin.

Post Viral Fatigue

Post viral fatigue, also known as ME is a syndrome which often follows a bad infection. The symptoms include chronic fatigue, depression and muscle weakness.

All of these illnesses give symptoms which could mask or be masked by those of SAD. However, none of them displays a seasonal nature. None of them would regularly start in the autumn and end in the spring year after year. The real feature which distinguishes SAD from other seemingly similar illnesses is the fact that SAD occurs in autumn and winter and is relieved in spring and summer. As we will see in the self-help SAD programme in Part Three, when making a diagnosis, it is essential to be aware of the seasonal nature of this illness. But before considering diagnosis of the syndrome, it is first necessary to look at who is likely to suffer from SAD and why.

WHO SUFFERS FROM SAD?

Since the early 1980s doctors in different countries have been investigating who suffers from SAD. The research started at the National Institute for Mental Health (NIMH) in the USA where, one winter, a research scientist called Herb admitted himself to the psychiatric clinic suffering from depression. Herb had experienced severe mood swings for thirty years, and over this time had become aware of a seasonal pattern to his symptoms. He noticed that each year between the middle and end of summer he became depressed and anxious. He found it difficult to mix with people or work efficiently. In addition, he was sleeping badly and couldn't get up in the morning. He had a tendency to eat more and put on weight as the winter progressed. When discussing his symptoms with psychiatrists at the NIMH, Herb complained that each autumn his depression, fatigue and lack of confidence led to a dramatic fall in his productivity at work. Yet when spring arrived his confidence increased, he became less tired and his energy and productivity soared. In fact by mid-spring Herb went into a manic state of hyperactivity, where he could only sleep for two or three hours per night.

Herb was aware of the fact that his mood was influenced by the seasonal shortening or lengthening of the days. He approached the doctors and researchers at the NIMH with the hunch that his mood swings were something to do with the changes in daylight experienced in winter. At the NIMH, two psychiatrists, Drs Lewy and Rosenthal, had already been investigating the effects of bright artificial light on mood and activity in animals and humans. They took up Herb's suggestion that he needed more daylight and suggested that bright artificial light be used to extend his dull winter days. As a result, they advised him to spend six hours each day sitting in front of a specially designed box which produced a very similar light to natural daylight. After three days of treatment Herb noticed a dramatic change in mood. His depression lifted and his energy returned. He began to behave as if it were spring.

Herb was the first patient to be treated for SAD. His hunch about the relationship between light and winter depression led to a series of clinical trials and investigations in many countries of the world: in the USA, England, Switzerland, Scandinavia, Germany, Japan, Australia, Canada, Soviet Union and India. Doctors keen to research the illness further published articles about the syndrome in newspapers and magazines in order to encourage anyone suffering from the symptoms to admit themselves to clinics for treatment. A detailed questionnaire was used to ascertain how many seasons of SAD these people had experienced, what their symptoms were, and the time of year these symptoms occurred. Those with SAD were accepted for treatment and their mood and behaviour were followed up over several years.

Despite minor differences, the results of observations from

different parts of the world agree that SAD strikes regardless of race, class or occupation. The disorder is found in both the northern and southern hemisphere and is particularly widespread in countries far from the equator, where winter brings long, dark nights and shorter daylight hours. The onset of the syndrome was found to always coincide with the decrease in daylight hours that occurs in autumn: in the northern hemisphere, this is around October; in the southern hemisphere, where the seasons are reversed, in May. The following graphs show the relationship between daylight hours and the onset and severity of SAD in both hemispheres.

As is shown by these graphs, the worst months for SAD in countries of the northern hemisphere, such as the USA, Europe, Scandinavia, and the Soviet Union, are November, December, January and February. But in countries of the southern hemisphere, such as Australia and New Zealand, the worst months are May, June, July and August.

SAD afflicts both sexes, but so far greater numbers of women sufferers have been identified than men. Onset of the symptoms generally begins around the second or third decade of life, that is in the patient's twenties and thirties, although, the illness has been diagnosed in some older adults and a small number of children and adolescents.

Many people who suffer from SAD come from a family with a history of the ailment. Alternatively, one of their immediate relatives is likely to have suffered some other form of depressive illness.

To summarize, some predisposing factors are:

- People living in areas far from the equator
- Women
- Those aged 20–40 years
- Those with a parent or close relative suffering SAD or other mood disorder

Such research gives a general picture of who suffers from

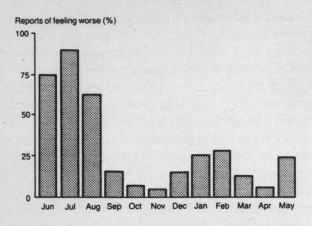

Reports of feeling worse (%)

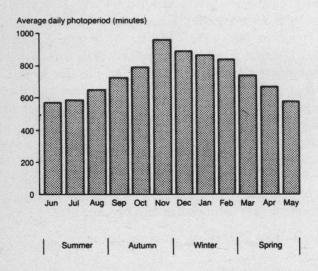

Average daily photoperiod (minutes)

| Summer | Autumn | Winter | Spring |

Frequency of individuals reporting 'feeling worse' for each month of the year in Melbourne, Australia correlates to the shortening of the daily photoperiod.

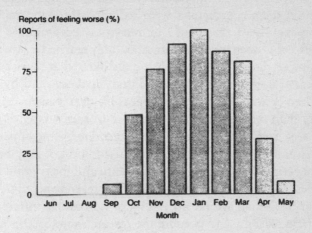

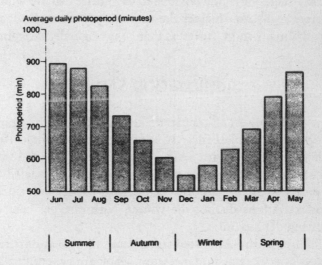

Frequency of subjects experiencing depression for each month of the year in Rockville, USA correlates to the shortening of the daily photoperiod.

SAD. However, the findings have their limitations. Most of the patients studied in the many research programmes used to draw these conclusions were recruited through articles in newspapers and magazines or television programmes. It is possible that such media information only reached a small proportion of the real sufferers. It is quite likely that more articles appeared in women's magazines than in those read by men, children or adolescents. It is also possible that women are more likely than men to admit to suffering from a winter disorder and seek help. These factors might account for the apparently larger number of female sufferers. In addition, it may be that more people between the ages of twenty and thirty would take interest in and follow up an article or television programme about SAD than would an elderly or adolescent sufferer. For all these reasons, and because the research into SAD is still in its early stages, it is not possible to categorize exactly who the sufferers really are. In fact the most recent research suggests there are many more sufferers than was originally thought.

CHILDHOOD SAD

Some SAD sufferers report that their condition began in childhood or adolescence. It is now becoming increasingly evident that adults with SAD often have children who suffer.

A survey carried out at a Minnesota school revealed that six per cent of the children claimed to experience extreme mood variations during the winter, with one per cent also reporting depression.

Children with SAD often suffer from fatigue and irritability, but not necessarily depression. They are generally aware that something is wrong, but are rarely conscious of a seasonal pattern. They see their problems stemming from external factors – the fact that a school teacher is picking on them, or their homework is too hard. Their symptoms are easily misdiagnosed or, in the case of teenagers, dismissed as the teething problems of adolescence. It is thus important to watch children carefully during the winter, noting if they experience a seasonal decline in academic achievement, activity or mood. Here is an example of one SAD child:

EMILY (13 years)

Emily's parents had not taken much notice of their daughter's symptoms at first. As a small child she had often suffered from colds during the winter, and they presumed this was the reason for her fatigue and lack of interest in school. However, after about her tenth birthday they began to notice that her mood changed in the winter regardless of whether she had a cold or not. She became markedly irritable with her younger sisters and often retired to her bedroom early in the evening, where she would lie on the bed dozing or gazing into space. Several times Emily's mother found her lying on her bed sobbing for no apparent reason. She was often reluctant to do her homework, practise the piano or even read a book. Although she went to bed early, Emily was always hard to rouse in the morning and often did not want to go to school.

Despite the Christmas festivities, Emily's parents noticed that their child's mood deteriorated throughout the rest of the winter, then suddenly as spring arrived she would perk up. She started to take an interest in her former activities: she practised the piano for several hours at a time, played with her sisters and seemed keen once again to accompany her mother on outings and invite friends home.

Almost all children with SAD suffer the following symptoms during the autumn and/or winter months:

- sadness
- anxiety
- irritability

SOME ALSO EXPERIENCE:

- fatigue
- sleep problems, disturbed sleep, tendency to fall asleep during the day
- increase in appetite
- carbohydrate or junk food cravings
- headaches

DIFFICULTIES AT SCHOOL:

- decline in academic achievements
- loss of desire to take part in activities, especially sports
- memory impairment
- poor organizational skills
- difficulty writing

BEHAVIOURAL DIFFICULTIES:

- withdrawal from family and friends
- crying spells
- temper tantrums
- tendency to watch a lot of television without retaining what is seen
- in springtime become hypomanic with feelings of elation, talkativeness, sleepless nights and hyperactivity.

Children's learning and behavioural problems can sometimes be attributed to SAD. Difficulty concentrating or keeping still, and low achievement may be diagnosed as attention deficit disorder and treated as such. However, similar problems sometimes occur in children with SAD. It is important to monitor a child's symptoms closely to see if they occur all year round, or if they appear only between October and May. If the child is evidently better during the summer months, and deteriorates in the winter, it is possible that light treatment may be helpful. It is advisable to seek professional help in establishing a diagnosis from a psychiatrist or psychologist.

Children have been treated for SAD in a similar way to adults. In the self help programme we will look at how treatment is successfully carried out.

HOW MANY PEOPLE SUFFER FROM SAD?

In Britain doctors so far have estimated that around five per cent of the population are SAD sufferers, that is one person in twenty. The same figure has been estimated for Australia

The following chart and map will help locate areas far from the equator where the incidence of SAD is likely to be high. In areas near the equator incidence of SAD is low.

LATITUDE	CITY/COUNTRY/STATE
60-65 N	Norway, Finland, Iceland, Alaska
55-60 N	Scotland, Russia, Denmark, Sweden
50-55 N	England, Ireland, Wales, Holland, northern and eastern Germany, Poland, western Canada
45-50 N	Switzerland, eastern Canada, Romania, Austria, Hungary, northern Italy, France, far northern USA (Washington, Montana, Dakota, Wisconsin)
40-45 N	Southern France, northern Spain, southern Italy, Yugoslavia, northern USA (New England, Midwest, Oregon)
35-40 N	Southern Spain, northern Africa, Turkey, Greece, northern China, Japan, central USA (California, Colorado, Carolina)

In areas between 30 degrees north and south of the equator few incidences of SAD are found.

30-35 S	South Africa, Sydney, Uruguay
35-40 S	Southern Australia, New Zealand, Argentina, Tasmania

and Canada. In the USA the figure is six per cent, or eleven million people.

The above figures have been estimated on the basis of people seeking help in response to medical surveys and magazine and newspaper articles. More recent random surveys have looked at the incidence of seasonal depression in the population at large and have come up with some astounding results.

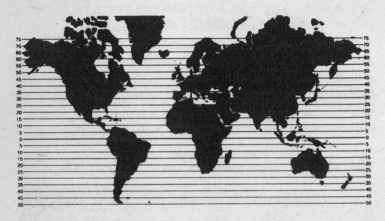

The incidence of SAD increases the further you are from the equator.

In a random telephone survey of the general population in Maryland, USA, it was revealed that ninety-two per cent of those interviewed about their reaction to winter (changes in mood, sleep duration, appetite, weight, energy and social activity) noticed seasonal changes. Twenty seven per cent considered these changes to be a problem in their lives, and between five and ten per cent rated a degree of seasonal difficulties equivalent to that of SAD patients. A similar survey in New York City showed up to twenty-five per cent of people with problematic symptoms in winter associated with weight gain, increased sleep duration and decreased social activity.

In a more extensive survey carried out over the eastern

United States, it was seen that incidence of SAD symptoms decreased with latitude. Fewer people suffered in southern states such as Florida, compared with New Hampshire, for example. These results lend support to the observation that SAD symptoms are often alleviated during a visit to southern locations.

THE DIFFERENT FACES OF SAD

The results of the survey carried out in the USA suggest that a large percentage of the population notices seasonal changes of some sort. This suggests that SAD is just one end of a spectrum of disorders ranging from mild, inconsequential effects through to increasingly problematic changes.

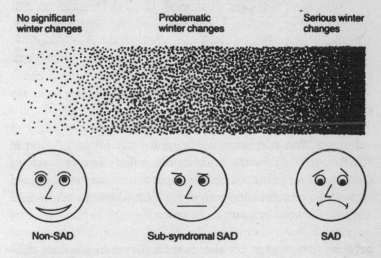

No significant winter changes

Problematic winter changes

Serious winter changes

Non-SAD

Sub-syndromal SAD

SAD

People who suffer mild symptoms of SAD are said to have 'sub-syndromal SAD'. Their symptoms can be any of those described above but to a lesser degree. In Britain and the United States, studies have shown that between 10 and 20 per cent of the population suffers from sub-syndromal SAD.

Sub-syndromal SAD generally begins later in winter and finishes earlier in spring than the more acute syndrome. Here is an example:

JACKIE:

I dislike the winter. As soon as the nights start to draw in I instinctively want to stay inside cosy and warm. When the clocks change that's it: getting up in the morning is an ordeal, I feel so tired and groggy; sometimes I don't even hear my alarm, I am so fast asleep.

I carry on more or less as normal, but as the winter goes on I seem to get more and more tired. I am never really full of energy or enthusiasm. I tend to avoid going out much in the winter evenings, preferring to curl up next to the fire to watch the television or read a good book.

I wouldn't say I get depressed, but I do get fed up and irritable with the cold, the wet and the darkness. I get round it by trying to relax more and to do things I enjoy. We generally get in a stock of good videos, books and music. I browse over holiday brochures to try and cheer myself up.

As for food, I always put on weight in the winter, it's inevitable. I go for thick soups, steak and kidney pie, and desserts. But at least in winter you wear plenty of clothes to disguise the extra weight, it's not as if you have to expose yourself in a bikini. I have a pre-summer diet and exercises which I follow in the spring which generally gets rid of the weight I put on in winter.

These are some of the symptoms common to sub-syndromal SAD which are evident for a short period during the height of winter:

- more sleep needed
- difficulties getting up in the morning

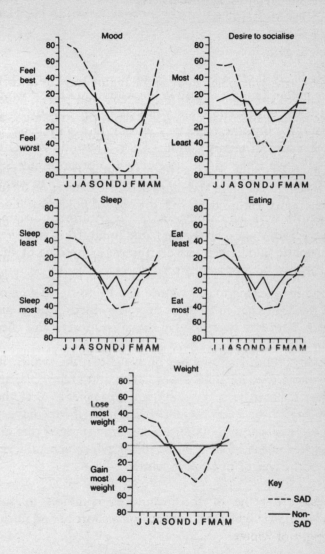

Seasonal rhythms of mood, diet, weight, sleep and sociability in SAD sufferers and non-SAD sufferers (northern hemisphere).

- extreme tiredness and listlessness
- carbohydrate cravings
- increased appetite
- weight gain

It is likely that at least some of the symptoms outlined above will be familiar to you in the winter months. You may barely notice their effects, or you may experience them in a very mild form; alternatively you may find they make the winter a time of misery and inactivity. The following chapters will give some of the reasons why doctors think SAD occurs, and why it affects some people more than others. Later, in the self help programme you can learn how to distinguish between chronic SAD, sub-syndromal SAD and other everyday seasonal changes, and finally look at how the problematic and sometimes destructive symptoms of these illnesses can be successfully treated.

2

From Hibernation to Depression

We have now established the classic symptoms of SAD: depression, a desire to sleep, eat and withdraw during the winter months. Such symptoms seem surprisingly similar to the behaviour of an animal in the throes of hibernation. Indeed, if we look at the reactions of animals, we can see that they have cyclical rhythms which are dictated by the seasons, just as the symptoms of SAD in humans appear to be. These biological rhythms in animals allow each species to survive in constantly changing seasonal conditions. This excerpt from 'The Wind in the Willows' gives an idea of how similar the symptoms of SAD are to the winter behaviour of some hibernating animals:

The badger went through a bit of hard thinking. 'Now look here!' he said at last rather severely; 'of course you know I can't do anything now?'

His two friends assented, quite understanding his point. No animal, according to the rules of animal etiquette, is ever expected to do anything strenuous, heroic, or even moderately active during the off-season of winter. All are sleepy – some actually asleep. All are weather-bound, more or less; and all are resting from arduous days and nights, during which every muscle in them has been severely tested, and every energy kept at full stretch.

'Very well then!' continued the Badger. 'But, when once the year has really turned and the nights are shorter, and halfway through them one rouses and feels fidgety and wanting to be up and doing by sunrise, if not before – you know!'

Both animals nodded gravely. They knew!

Annual hibernation is perfectly natural in a badger or a squirrel. But when humans start to demonstrate similar tendencies it is considered unacceptable. Many SAD patients compare themselves to animals when describing how they feel. 'I wish I were a hedgehog and could just roll up in the leaves and go to sleep', said one sufferer to me. Unlike the badger, it is unacceptable for her to eat, sleep and do nothing all winter. Instead, she has a family to look after, a job to do, people to see. One of the problems SAD sufferers face in today's society is the constant need to fight against their symptoms.

We tend to think that seasonal cycles of behaviour and bodily functions are reserved for animals living off the land. We assume that the influence of the seasons on humans died with our Stone Age ancestors. Humans today, in heated and artificially lit buildings, exist regardless of the climatic extremes and seasonal variabilities experienced by our forefathers.

However, as research looks further into the underlying causes of SAD, it brings to light the fact that even today, in a world alienated from the natural habitat of animals, humans still function according to the seasons. New findings suggest that our indoor life, which cuts us off from external seasonal conditions, in particular daylight, may be harmful to our health and well being.

HOW DO SEASONAL RHYTHMS WORK?

Seasonal rhythms in sexual activity, hibernation and migratory behaviour are widespread among animals and birds.

These rhythms enable members of a species to synchronize their activities with respect to one another and to the demands of the environment. For example, lambs are born only in the spring when there is plentiful food for the mother to nurse the newborn. In fact most species coordinate their mating time so that birth occurs in the season when the most food will be available. Birds may also take nest availability into consideration. In the tropical rainforests, for example, birds generally wait for the dry season to breed, while in the Arctic, breeding appears to be timed, at least in part, to coincide with the melting of snow and ice.

Such activities indicate that animals function according to the demands of the seasons. They also suggest that animals have advance knowledge of which season will be appropriate for which activities. How do animals and birds synchronize their mating habits in order to conceive at the appropriate moment when food and shelter will be available? How do birds know when to start preparing for migration in order to store enough energy to last them the journey? Do they have advance warning that the season is going to change, a sort of internal weather forecast?

Changes in temperature play an important role in determining animal and bird behavioural patterns, but the fact that temperatures can at times be erratic and deceiving (an Indian summer or a late spring frost, for example) means that they are not the most important factor. Instead, most animals synchronize their patterns of behaviour by the number of hours of daylight they experience, otherwise known as the photoperiod.

For example, in animals which mate only at certain seasons of the year, the photoperiod acts as a trigger or signal: the amount of daylight the female is exposed to determines the activation of hormones which allow the release of an egg for fertilization; in the male the length of photoperiod prepares the testicles for the production of sperm.

Daylight plays a vital part in initiating responses in animals because among all obvious environmental stimuli it is the most reliable. Almost all classes of activities found to occur in animals on a seasonal basis are influenced by the number of daylight hours.

LIGHT CONTROLS HUMAN FUNCTIONS

It is not just animals and birds which function according to the photoperiod. The biological rhythms of humans are also influenced to some extent. The number of hours of daylight we experience tells us both the time of day or night and the time of year. The photoperiod influences our daily, monthly and annual cycles of sleeping, eating and reproduction. This is because light stimulates or suppresses the secretion of hormones regulating these cycles. For examples, have you ever wondered why we start to feel sleepy when it is dark and more awake with the morning light? One of the most obvious examples of the way light controls both animal and human habits and functioning is its effect on the hormonal system in regulating a cycle of sleeping and waking. In most animals the desire to sleep is brought on by secretion of a hormone called melatonin. Melatonin is produced in a tiny gland at the base of the brain. It is known as the pineal gland, because it resembles a pine cone, yet it is about the size of a pea. In the evening the pineal gland reacts to the diminishing levels of daylight and starts to produce melatonin, which is then released into the blood and flows through the body making us drowsy. Its secretion peaks in the middle of the night during our heaviest hours of sleep. In the morning, bright light shining through the eye reaches the pineal gland which reacts by switching off the production of melatonin, thus removing the desire to sleep.

The pineal gland is linked up to the rest of the hormonal

system. Consequently melatonin production also influences the functioning of other parts of the body. During darkness and sleep, melatonin modifies the secretion of hormones from organs such as the pituitary, the master gland of the hormonal system. The pituitary in turn regulates the secretion of hormones controlling growth, milk production, egg and sperm production. It also regulates the action of the thyroid gland, which is concerned with metabolism, and the adrenal glands, which control excretion of the body's waste. It is obvious then that fluctuations in light and darkness according to the seasons of the year will influence rhythms of growth, reproduction and activity in animals and indeed humans.

Light, then, plays a major role in controlling many of the body's systems. Its influence is more obvious if we consider how early man probably lived his life. As a hunter and fisher he would have been forced to adapt to the constraints placed on him by the seasonal changes in the hours of daylight. The winter darkness and low temperatures allowed little activity, consequently it would have been regarded as a time to rest, conserve energy and withdraw. Spring and summer, when the hours of light were at their longest, was the peak time for procuring food. If we look at primitive hunting and fishing tribes which exist today, we can still see definite seasonal patterns of behaviour relating to climate and photoperiod. For example, the Mongoloid Yakaghir, in East Siberia, limit their serious hunting to times of maximum daylight and optimum temperature: the autumn and spring; summer is a time to relax and hold games, and winter a period of withdrawal. Eskimos, the last surviving hunter-fishers of the New World, also have seasonal patterns of activity. In the summer they disperse in family groups to hunt whale and seals. With the approach of autumn they settle down to fishing through holes in the ice. During the two darkest months of the winter, life is confined to the permanent settlements where several families live together and draw on stores of food accumulated

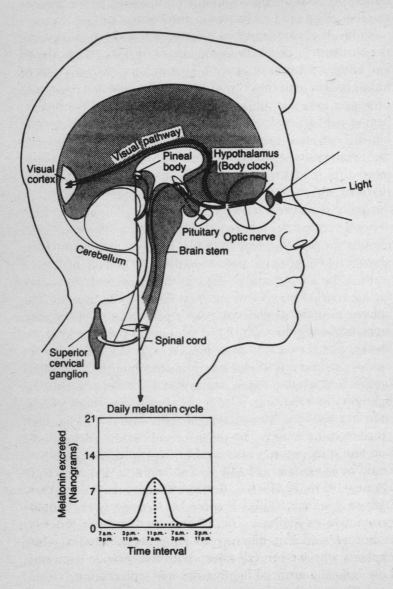

The influence of light on the production of melatonin.

during previous months. Spring, with its return of the sun, is traditionally a time for courtship and conception.

Today, the majority of us no longer live close enough to the elements to be aware of the effects of light on our daily and annual patterns of activity. First gas and then electricity have brought a means of transforming the cold and darkness of winter into warmth and light. We are shielded from the heat and brightness of spring and summer by tinted glass, blinds, and air conditioning. Some of us spend most of our living hours in conditions of artificial lighting. Does this mean that modern man is totally immune to the seasonal rhythms and the variability in photoperiod experienced by our more primitive ancestors?

Recent research has shown that this is not the case. Despite the fact that electricity allows us to manipulate our activities so that we are not constrained to sleep at dusk and wake at dawn, we are still dependent on natural sunlight for the regulation of many of the body's functions. Artificial lighting provides us with enough light to continue reading or working during the night, but it does not necessarily keep us awake. The reason for this is that the type of indoor lighting we use is not of sufficient intensity to affect the hormonal mechanisms which control our bodily rhythms. Intensity of light is measured in lux. This is the standard measure which indicates the received intensity of light at a particular distance from its source. The electric light used in most homes and workplaces rarely exceeds 500 lux. A sunny afternoon could be as much as 100,000 lux, and even the cloudiest day is rarely below 10,000 lux. Researchers have discovered that light of at least 2,500 lux is necessary to suppress melatonin production in humans. The artificial light we use indoors is not of sufficient intensity to suppress melatonin. This explains why we can fall asleep with the bedside lamp on. Low intensity artificial lighting has not replaced our bodies need for natural daylight.

Statistics show that despite our enclosed habitat, our bodies still respond to the external environment and to its seasonal variability in duration and intensity. Research carried out since the turn of the century has confirmed that growth rates in children are affected by the seasons: surveys carried out in Germany, Sweden and Scotland show that height and weight increase in the spring and early summer. Studies have shown that in many countries the rate of conception peaks in the summer when the hours of daylight are longest. In numerous trials the seasons have been seen to influence the timing and duration of sleep, pain threshold, alertness, eating habits, mood, the onset of menstruation in women and sexual activity.

BIOLOGICAL CLOCKS

Despite the obvious role light plays in the body's functioning, large numbers of people in modern society are deprived of natural sunlight. They spend most of their waking hours in artificial light of low intensity. How then are their daily and annual rhythms able to sustain their activity in the absence of sufficient daylight?

Experiments have been carried out on animals placed in static lighting conditions to assess whether their seasonal rhythms are inhibited by the lack of seasonal fluctuations in daylight. It was thought that if squirrels were blinded, their inability to assimilate light would disrupt their seasonal cycle of hibernation. But no, at the appropriate time of year the blinded animals prepared for hibernation, regardless of their inability to assimilate light. The same was found in birds which demonstrate a seasonal moult. When the birds were totally deprived of the light the moult still occurred at around the appropriate season. In fact up to thirty different species have now been tested under static environmental conditions, and the results have shown that functions as diverse as hibernation, migratory behaviour, and milk production continue to function in a regular cyclical manner despite the absence of light variability.

Similar tests have been carried out on humans to establish how their daily cycles function in the absence of natural daylight. Experiments where humans were placed in isolation chambers, cut off from all potential environmental cues, have shown similar results to the experiments carried out on animals: that is, in the absence of natural daylight, rhythms are maintained, but over a period which deviates from the exact time of the rhythms experienced under natural conditions. Daily cycles, for example became slightly longer than 24 hours. Scientists have described these approximate daily rhythms as 'circadian' from the Latin words circa: about, and dies: days. Approximate yearly rhythms have been called 'circannual' rhythms. The discovery that animals and humans can continue to function according to daily and annual rhythms in the absence of external environmental stimuli suggests that their seasonal rhythms do not just run according to the daily variation in light, but are operated by some sort of internal biological clocks, which run independently, regardless of whether we are indoors or outside.

In the case of animals, these clocks act as a back up system, should environmental conditions fail to let animals know the time of day or season. This is helpful, as even daylight can be unpredictable: cloud can obscure a bright day giving the impression of autumn in mid-summer, for example. If animals relied totally on environmental conditions they would experience a considerable year-to-year variability in the timing of their activities, which would not necessarily be to their benefit.

But this does not mean that light, food supply, and climatic conditions are irrelevant in determining the rhythms of animals and humans. Although there is no doubt that an inbuilt body clock regulates approximate daily, monthly and annual rhythms, light and other external influences help in the exact synchronization of these rhythms, bringing them into line with the natural year and 24-hour day. In other words, natural daylight helps the clocks keep the 'exact time' rather than the 'approximate time'. It is thought that the cyclical functions of both animals and humans operate through a combination of mechanisms: inbuilt body clocks working in collaboration with external seasonal influences, in particular the light-dark cycle.

The presence of circadian and circannual rhythms explains how humans can manage, in the absence of environmental stimuli, to sustain a range of biological rhythms, such as growth, reproduction, sleeping and waking, appetite and metabolism, amongst others. Despite living and working in artificially lit, heated and air conditioned dwellings, it is possible to maintain a certain regularity of circadian and circannual rhythms with the help of our internal biological clocks.

However, in the absence of natural light our body clocks may lose or gain a little time. This in turn could lead to the desynchronization of different rhythms. For example, in the absence of sufficient environmental light the sleep-wake and associated rest-activity rhythms may lengthen to a cycle of between 30 and 48 hours, while the temperature rhythm may remain at a period of, say, 25 hours. Such desynchronization of the body's intricate rhythms is suspected to trigger problems: hormonal imbalances, sleep disorders and mood disturbances.

Just as animals rely on signals from the sun to keep their body clocks exact and to synchronize their activities, so humans need sufficient daylight to synchronize their circadian and circannual rhythms. It has been suggested that a number of illnesses which result from hormonal imbalances – sleep, appetite, mood and reproductive disorders – could be linked to a disruption of circadian rhythms and ultimately to a lack of sufficient sunlight. SAD is an example of disturbed sleep patterns, appetite and weight disorders and depression, all of which manifest in a yearly and daily cycle: the symptoms peak at the height of winter and are at their worst in the evening. Giving SAD patients artificial daylight has proved successful in correcting these disorders, which suggests that SAD is directly associated with a lack of sufficient light.

SAD is not the only illness to demonstrate evidence or circadian rhythm disturbances. Classical depression exhibits a daily rhythm which worsens in the morning and improves in the evening, presenting mood swings, along with insomnia or disturbed sleep patterns. Today, classical depression is often treated with drugs which exert an influence on circadian rhythms, and doctors are looking at the possibility of treating it with light. Menstrual disturbances in women, such as irregular menstrual cycles or premenstrual syndrome are further examples of disturbances in the body's biological clocks. Again research is looking at the possibility of treatment with light.

The link between the absence of sunlight, a disruption in circadian rhythms and illness has been established. In the case of SAD, this link has been particularly valuable in providing effective and safe treatment. The next chapter will look at how this link was made and explain the current theories on why phototherapy is an effective treatment for SAD.

3

Seeing the Light

The discovery that the brain controls itself and the rest of the body by some sort of internal biological clock was a major breakthrough in psychiatric research. Now doctors also know that the regularity of this clock is sustained by daily and seasonal changes in duration and intensity of daylight. This finding has had promising implications for the treatment of disorders thought to be related to a disturbance in the circadian rhythm system. It suggests that manipulations of patients' exposure to sunlight could permit such disturbances to be rectified. Research is being carried out to investigate this potential treatment in patients suffering depression and sleep disorders and, in particular, SAD.

The use of light therapy to treat SAD was started at the National Institute for Mental Health (NIMH). The seemingly magical cure which occurred in Herb, the first patient there, aroused much interest in winter depression. However, Herb was a single case. It was necessary to test the light therapy on other people and to try to establish why it relieved the winter symptoms of fatigue, appetite increase and depression. Doctors at the NIMH thus started to treat groups of patients who demonstrated recurrent winters of SAD symptoms.

Early researchers of SAD came to the conclusion that the reason patients were suffering from winter depression was that they were deprived of sufficient daylight. Symptoms were made worse by the autumn and winter decrease in daylight hours. When in spring the days grew longer again the symptoms were relieved. Exposing patients to standard indoor lighting did not make any difference to the onset of the syndrome. On testing the intensity of the electric bulbs or fluorescent tubes which most people use to light their offices and homes during the day and during a large part of the evening, it was seen that they were not sufficiently bright to substitute the lack of natural daylight. Most indoor lighting used was equivalent to dim twilight only and thus did not play a part in sustaining the regularity of the body's internal clocks.

Initial experiments were carried out by placing winter depressed patients in front of an electric light box which emitted bright light of an intensity equivalent to that found outside on a spring day. The patients were given three hours of artificial light before dawn, and three after dusk, thus bringing their quota of hours of light up to the number experienced on a summer's day. Within four days of receiving this treatment the patients underwent a dramatic improvement. Their exhaustion was lifted, their desire to sleep too, and they no longer felt depressed. In fact they felt as if it was spring several months ahead of time.

At the same time as work was being carried out on the use of artificial light to treat SAD, doctors at the NIMH were also investigating the effect of a total absence of daily and seasonal environmental stimuli on humans. Their experiments consisted of placing people in isolation chambers of static lighting conditions to establish what happened to their daily rhythms in the absence of day and night. This work interested an English psychiatrist, Professor Thompson, who decided to visit the Institute for a month to look at the work being done on circadian rhythms. However, on arrival there he found that the experiments were not working out as planned. The conditions in which people were isolated were unsatisfactory for the experiments to be carried out, and hence Thompson was unable to pursue his observations as hoped. He had arranged to be at the Institute for one month, so it was at this point that be became fascinated by some much more inter-esting research which was being carried out.

Thompson became involved in the diagnosis and treatment of SAD patients seen at the Institute. He spent the whole month observing SAD cases, and on his return to Britain decided to continue the research at Charing Cross Hospital. His first step was to find SAD sufferers. He informed GPs and specialists of the syndrome and asked them to send him any patients they suspected might be suffering from SAD. His request met with some scepticism, and few referrals were made. So Thompson took the plunge and spoke to the press. Soon after, an article on SAD in London's Evening Standard brought a flood of letters from readers claiming to suffer the symptoms it described. As a result the first SAD clinic was established at Charing Cross Hospital. This opened the way to the successful treatment of hundreds of SAD sufferers and led to the opportunity to carry out research in Britain on how and why the illness occurs.

The news of SAD spread worldwide. Clinics were set up in many states of the USA, Canada, Switzerland, Germany, Norway, Australia, and Japan. In each country patients with the same symptoms were found and doctors began to publish the news of SAD and its treatment in newspapers and maga-zines. The publicity brought a constant stream of enquiries from many people who recognized in themselves the symptoms they were reading about. Such candidates were screened, by the use of a detailed questionnaire asking them about their symptoms, their medical and family history, and the effects of environmental changes on the severity of their condition. Of course not all were suffering from SAD, but of the ones who were, treatment was then offered.

SAD patients were treated with phototherapy in every country where studies were performed. And in seventy-five to eighty per cent of cases an improvement in symptoms occurred. Thus, it appeared that a cure had been found for most people with SAD. Yet, the reasons why that cure occurred were uncertain. However, an important step forward had been made: doctors had built up a clinical picture of the typical SAD patient, and his/her symptoms. The next step was to discover how light brought relief of symptoms, and why it occurred in some but not all patients.

The early patients at the NIMH, Charing Cross Hospital, and other clinics around the world were to some extent guinea pigs in research projects to ascertain how light therapy brings relief to SAD symptoms. They were given different types of light treatment at different times of the day in order to establish how light affects the body and which intensity of light is most effective in curing SAD and at what time. Such information gave doctors important clues in assessing the mechanism by which phototherapy cures SAD. The results of their clinical trials brought a number of different theories about the illness and the efficacy of treatment. Here are some of their findings.

Too Much Melatonin?

The idea of giving patients light in order to relieve winter symptoms of depression and fatigue had been developed at the NIMH as a result of experiments on animals. It had been noticed that bright light which was shone in the eyes of animals arrested the production of melatonin, the hormone which brings sleep. The same experiment was carried out on humans. Blood tests were taken in humans at regular intervals during the night and before and after shining bright light through the eye. It was noticed that after bright light melatonin levels in the blood of humans dropped rapidly. While melatonin could be suppressed in animals by light of very low intensity, it was discovered that humans needed light of much higher intensity, at least 2,500 lux to bring suppression. Thus the normal artificial indoor light to which humans are often exposed during the day and certainly during the evening is not bright enough to arrest melatonin production. It was assumed that during the winter when the evenings draw in and nights are longer, melatonin secretion commences earlier and finishes later in each 24-hour cycle. Doctors suggested that the reason SAD patients felt constantly tired and depressed was because the darker days of winter were causing them to produce abnormally high levels of melatonin, which in turn made them drowsy. The doctors suspected that excess melatonin production was also responsible for the mood and behavioural abnormalities found in SAD patients.

It was initially thought that light therapy acted on SAD patients by suppressing their abnormally high levels of melatonin and thus alleviating the imbalances in the hormonal system it caused. This theory was further substantiated when it was realized that if melatonin was fed to patients during light therapy, the light treatment did not relieve their symptoms.

However, if SAD were just a question of excess melatonin in the system, this could be resolved by drugs which prevent melatonin secretion, a much more convenient treatment than phototherapy. To test out this theory the doctors replaced light therapy with a drug called atenolol. This medication completely suppresses the secretion of melatonin and, it was hoped, would therefore have the same effect on SAD sufferers as light therapy. The patients' symptoms were assessed before and after light therapy. During treatment with atenolol the patients' blood was analysed at regular intervals to ensure that no melatonin was present. The results showed that atenolol had indeed prevented secretion of melatonin, but had not alleviated the SAD symptoms. Winter depression was evidently not purely a question of too much melatonin in the system.

Shorter Days

Some researchers suggested that light therapy worked by extending the daylight period. This theory was tested by

Professor Thompson at Charing Cross Hospital. In his study patients were consecutively treated with bright light of 2,500 lux morning and evening, dim light of insufficient intensity to influence melatonin secretion, and light of 2,500 lux for four hours during the middle of the day. The midday treatment would have no effect on melatonin production because the hormone is only secreted at night. The results of the tests showed that the dim and bright light administered morning and evening showed little differentiation in results. The treatment with midday light however showed a greater therapeutic effect. This study suggested that it is not necessary to artificially extend the day length or to suppress melatonin production to alleviate the symptoms of SAD. It is the amount and intensity of light that SAD patients receive each day, regardless of the time of day it is administered, which brings results, claimed Thompson.

A Disruption of Body Clocks?

Researchers started to look at the possibility that SAD patients suffer a disruption in the synchronization of their body clocks. They monitored the 24-hour rise and fall in melatonin levels in SAD patients and discovered that both the evening rise and the morning decline in melatonin levels occurred several hours earlier than in normal people. This suggested that the biological clock of SAD sufferers may be delayed, or running slow. By administering light early in the morning, this delay would be advanced and thus the disruption would be reversed. But, by the same theory, it follows that light therapy in the evening would cause a further delay in the clocks rhythm. However, when patients were given phototherapy in the evening rather than the morning or at midday, an improvement was also noticed. The effects of phototherapy were thus something other than a reversal of delayed biological clocks.

Hormonal Deficiency?

Doctors are now speculating that it is at the hypothalamus itself, the centre of the brain, where a deficiency may lie for those suffering from SAD. Although research is in its early stages, it is now thought that SAD patients may be deficient in the brain chemicals, serotonin and dopamine: two substances present in the hypothalamus, whose function it is to pass messages from one nerve cell to another.

It is known that lack of serotonin in the brain brings depression. It is also known that in the population as a whole, serotonin levels are at their lowest in winter. Eating carbohydrates boosts the production of serotonin; if SAD sufferers are deficient in serotonin, this may explain their desire to eat carbohydrates, especially sweet foods. Bright light appears to regulate serotonin deficiency, and this could be one of the reasons for the success of light therapy on SAD patients. Drugs which stimulate serotonin production have also been relatively successful in treating SAD.

Tests on SAD patients have revealed abnormalities in temperature regulation, rate of blinking and secretion of a pituitary hormone called prolactin. These functions all depend on a brain chemical called dopamine, which is also suspected to be deficient in the absence of sufficient bright light. Dopamine is present in the eye and is released in response to light. This again may account for the beneficial effects of light on SAD sufferers.

Light Sensitivity?

While the controversy over the mechanism of phototherapy continues, other researchers are now looking at the question of light assimilation: the way light is absorbed through the eyes. Perhaps SAD patients are less sensitive to light than the average person; they may have problems assimilating light, due to a defect in the eye or the nerves leading back to the brain. In order to assess this theory, vision tests were carried out that compared SAD patients and a non-SAD control group to ascertain differences of a physical or chemical nature in the tract leading from the eye to the pineal gland. The results showed there were no defects. SAD patients were perfectly able to assimilate light.

More recent research in Britain has however shown that light affects SAD sufferers differently from other people. Thompson has demonstrated that SAD patients are supersensitive to bright light, but only during the winter months. In his experiments two groups, one of twelve SAD patients and one of eleven non-SAD control subjects both received bright light and dim light between 12.30 pm and 1.30 am on consecutive nights. The experiment was carried out in winter and summer. As was expected, both groups responded to the bright light which brought a sharp drop in melatonin levels. Neither group responded to dim light. In the winter experiment a further observation was made: the SAD group experienced a far greater drop in melatonin in response to bright light than did the control group. In summer, however, the SAD group experienced a smaller drop in melatonin levels than did the non-SAD group in response to bright light. This experiment concludes that SAD sufferers are more sensitive to bright light in winter than people without SAD. However, in summer, SAD sufferers are less sensitive to light than the rest of the population.

Thompson believes that light sensitivity in SAD sufferers changes with the seasons. This may explain why SAD patients respond to bright light therapy in winter whereas classical depressives do not. It also suggests that SAD sufferers need more light in the winter than other non-SAD people do. Thompson claims that his experiments prove beyond doubt that SAD is not just an extreme dislike of winter, but is associated with measurable physical abnormalities in the body's complex system of assessing the time of day and year.

Dawn and Dusk Simulation?

Research in the USA has taken a different tack to that carried out in England. Dr Terman at the New York State Psychiatric Institute has been investigating why SAD patients experience a sudden and spontaneous recovery in the spring. Although dawn breaks earlier in New York in March than in December, it is not immediately clear why this should cause SAD sufferers to suddenly receive increased doses of light. After all, most of them are generally in bed asleep, not outside soaking up the sun. What spring does bring, is an earlier gradual dawn twilight in the bedroom, during sleep, which contrasts to the total darkness of winter mornings. This, Terman suspects, is significant to the sudden recovery SAD sufferers experience in the spring.

Terman's interest in the effects of gradual dawn light on mood and behaviour originated in his observation of animals. He noticed that the activity of animals is accelerated during light changes: for example, during the gradual change of light intensity which occurs at dawn, or the gradual dimming which occurs at dusk. During the winter this pattern changes markedly. This led Terman to suggest that the timing of dawn and dusk, with their gradual light changes, are more important to SAD sufferers than the overall intensity or quantity of light they receive.

To test this theory he devised an ambitious computer algorithm which predicts the intensity of light outdoors at any given time. It shows the continuous change in light intensity, from starlight, which is 1/10,000th lux, to bright daylight of 100,000 lux or more, at any given location. This device, which was placed beside the bed of SAD sufferers, was programmed to produce in winter the dawn light change which would normally be experienced in the bedroom at the beginning of spring. As the patient slept, the artificial light controller automatically switched on, and very dim light gradually built up to around 500 lux, imitating the natural onset of dawn which would filter through the curtains in springtime.

The patients were tested after one to two weeks of this treatment. Results showed that dawn simulation produces the same effects as the bright light therapy which had formerly been used during the day: it suppressed melatonin and reverted the delay in circadian rhythms. Moreover, the patients depression was lifted, and other symptoms of SAD relieved: patients did not oversleep, but woke spontaneously to the artificial spring dawn light with increased energy.

Terman then tried giving his patients artificial dusk twilight in the evening, and found that this produce a pleasant hypnotic sensation, which allowed them to fall asleep easier. The use of dawn and dusk simulation seemed to help in resolving poor sleep problems.

Dawn stimulation is now widely used. Research has shown that it is 75 per cent as effective as 10,000 lux light. The light levels are set much lower than the light box – at full between 100 lux and 1,700 lux. The dawn simulator is convenient as it is used while the patient is asleep and acts as a 'natural alarm clock'. As yet, the naturalistic twilight simulator necessary for this treatment is not available to the public, but it is successfully being used in trials in New York.

The most recent studies point to a link between light travelling through the eye, and the workings of the hypothalamus, a small but very important part of the brain that controls hormones governing mood, appetite, sleep, temperature and sex drive. Light enters the eye and causes impulses to travel along a nerve pathway, the retinohypothalamic tract, leading from the retina to the hypothalamus. When insufficient light enters the eye to stimulate neural action, or when there is a faulty mechanism in the retinohypothalamic tract, which slows down neural activity or prevents it, the hormonal activity in the hypothalamus decreases, along with the functions it regulates. This is thought to happen during the winter months in people who suffer from SAD.

Each year brings new discoveries about SAD and how to treat it. Still there is no concrete explanation of why some people suffer from it and others do not. However, what is clear, is that in the majority of patients (85 per cent of diagnosed cases) light therapy significantly relieves the symptoms of SAD. A vast number of medical studies carried out in most industrialized countries have supported the efficacy of phototherapy, yet the reasons why phototherapy brings relief to SAD sufferers are still a source of hot discussion. One of the reasons for this is the difficulty of carrying out research on mental illness. The brain is the most complex part of the human anatomy. Doctors can rarely delve inside it experimentally while patients are still living. They have to depend on experiments on animals or clinical trials on humans which are limited to behavioural observation and blood and urine sampling to ascertain changes in brain and body chemistry.

Clinical trials demand patience and meticulous attention to detail. Every experiment must be tested against a control group which receives a placebo, that is an illusion of treatment, but not the real thing. In clinical trials for drugs, control groups are given sugar pills as placebos. In the case of phototherapy, control groups may be given as a placebo light of a different intensity than that which is known to cure SAD. Despite the use of control studies, the findings of such experiments are often conflicting. Owing to the power of expectation that a treatment will work, some patients respond favourably to placebo treatment, hence complicating the research.

Despite these difficulties, doctors have reached basic conclusions concerning SAD and its treatment. Essentially the lack of available light in the winter is thought to precipitate winter depression. Replacement light of high intensity provided by phototherapy cures it. As research continues to determine how and why such treatment works, more effective and convenient methods of phototherapy will emerge that can be used to treat not only SAD, but also other related illnesses.

4

Light Starvation

Seasonal affective disorder is not the only illness known to be caused by lack of sunlight. Neither is it the first to be treated with artificial light. Despite the uncertainty surrounding the mechanism of treatment for SAD, there is no doubt that light is a vital nutrient to plant, animal and human life, and that deprivation can cause ill health. As scientists uncover more facts about the effects of light on the human body, it becomes more obvious that by enclosing ourselves in buildings with substandard illumination we run the risk of jeopardizing our well being and perhaps becoming physically ill.

It is common knowledge that without light the eye cannot see. Light provides us with an essential visual source. What are often forgotten however, are the other roles light plays in the body; as it passes through the skin or eyes to the body's hormonal system.

A glowing and bronzed skin is one of the most obvious of the body's reactions to sunlight. Sunlight shining on the skin initiates the production of melanin. Not to be confused with melatonin, melanin is a dark pigment which thickens and protects the body's surface. The darkness of our skin depends on the production of melanin. The skin of a black African, for example, has more melanin than a blonde northern European. As ultra violet rays from the sun penetrate the skin's surface layer of melanin, the body's store of vitamin D is replenished. The vitamin subsequently passes into the blood stream and makes its way to the kidneys and liver where it plays an essential role in allowing the absorption of calcium from foods which is then used to build and repair bones and teeth.

Light passing through the eyes performs very different functions. It allows us to see, by entering the visual pathway. But, as we have seen in previous chapters, it also takes another route through the brain to the hypothalamus, and then to the pineal gland, where it exerts its influence on the regulation of hormonal and neurochemical functions in the rest of the body. Through these mechanisms light plays a subtle role in organizing the body's biological daily, monthly and yearly rhythms.

INADEQUATE LIGHTING

Light thus has many roles to play in the body, but these roles can only be fulfilled if we receive the correct type of lighting: that which has the ultra violet rays which can penetrate the skin to produce vitamin D, and light of sufficient intensity to regulate the hormonal mechanisms of the body. Unfortunately most indoor artificial lighting is deficient in both. Despite the results of research showing the vital roles light plays on the regulation of mechanisms other than sight, architects, engineers and interior designers rarely look further than our visual needs when considering the provision of lighting in workplaces and homes. Their aim is to provide adequate illumination in which to work or read, in a way that is energy and cost efficient. In some cases attempts are made to offer sophisticated fittings, shades and lighting effects, but with aesthetic appeal in mind, not health. The effects of light on the biological functions of the body are generally ignored.

As a result, the artificial lighting used inside most buildings today differs significantly from the natural sunlight outside. It differs both in intensity and the range of colours it provides. Although invisible to the eye, natural daylight is made up of a relatively even distribution of all the colours of the spectrum, that is the colours of the rainbow. In fact, it is precisely the splitting of light into its constituent colours by water droplets in clouds that creates the rainbow effect. In contrast, most artificial lights provide a more uneven mixture of colours.

The most familiar type of artificial light is that generated by the common electric light bulb. This passes electricity through a metal filament to produce heat. When the temperature reaches 500 degrees C (943 degrees F) the filament begins to give off light as well as heat. The light generated is adequate to see with, but is quite different from the light of the sun. This is because most of the energy that an electric bulb uses is wasted in producing infrared radiation (heat), only about six per cent of the energy input is used to produce light. Consequently it emits a lot of red rays, but very few violet, blue and green.

Fluorescent strip lighting, popular in offices, factories and shops for its economy of energy and installation, operates by another mechanism altogether. It offers yet another variety of light which also differs from that generated by the sun. Within the glass tube of a fluorescent lamp, ultra violet rays are generated by a mercury vapour arc. The tube is lined with specially designed luminescent compounds which when hit by the ultra violet rays emit light of certain colours. Which colours are emitted depends on the type of compounds used to line the tube. Generally these tubes are designed to give off a high level of yellow-green light, the colours to which the eye is most sensitive. Thus they offer a seemingly very bright light while using relatively little energy. However, like the incandescent bulbs, their light is significantly different to that of the sun.

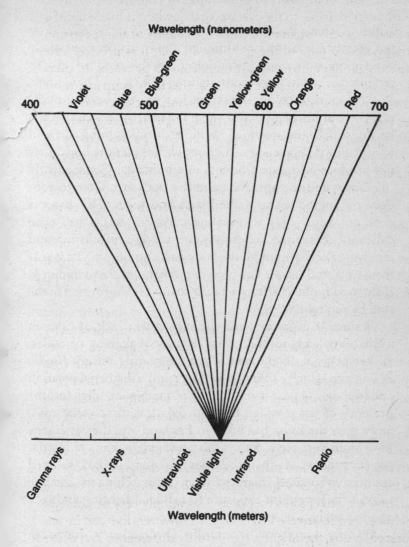

The position of visible light in the electromagnetic spectrum.

VITAMIN D DEFICIENCY

Lighting which has an uneven distribution of colours does not greatly impair vision, although it may distort our colour perception somewhat: incandescent bulbs tend to give a reddish hue, while fluorescent lighting gives a cold blue tinge. The incomplete colour spectrum has more severe implications on our health than our sight. It has been shown that the lack of sufficient ultra violet rays in artificial lighting can lead to nutritional deficiencies. Without ultra violet the body does not produce adequate amounts of vitamin D. Consequently calcium cannot be absorbed and the body is unable to produce the ingredient to make bones and teeth. This process does not apply only to growing children: adults too need calcium because the skeleton is constantly reproducing and renewing itself. Although the body can also obtain vitamin D from milk and fish, it has been demonstrated that vitamin D from food is not as effective biologically as that formed in the skin by sunlight.

Vitamin D deficiency and the subsequent lack of calcium availability leads to malformation and weakening of bones. Rickets is generally thought of as a nineteenth century disease in England which caused bowed legs and a distorted pelvis in children. In the past it resulted from inadequate diet and the presence of smog which blocked the vital ultra violet rays. Since then the smog has lifted in England and dietary habits have improved, but rickets is still prevalent in many industrial societies today. Many of the cases are found in dark-skinned children who have migrated from sunny climates and are faced with long-term exposure to artificial lighting and lack of adequate sunlight.

Another symptom of vitamin D deficiency, found in adults, is osteomalacia or a softening of the bones. A study conducted at the Mineral Metabolism Unit of the General Infirmary in Leeds showed more frequent signs of

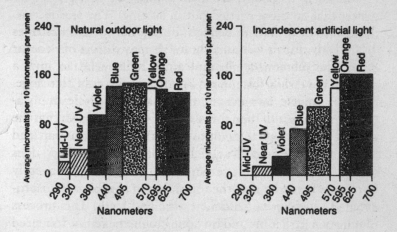

The spectral distribution of outdoor light compared with an incandescent lamp. Incandescent light has a heavier weighting of red light than natural daylight.

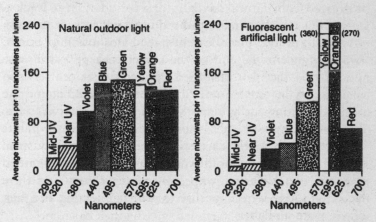

The spectral distribution of outdoor light compared with a fluorescent lamp. Fluorescent light has a heavier weighting of blue or green and yellow light (see above) than natural daylight which has an equal balance of these colours.

osteomalacia in post mortem examinations carried out in winter than in those carried out in summer. The reason was thought to be the lack of sunlight during the winter months.

The lack of adequate sunlight for the production of vitamin D and the subsequent metabolism of calcium is also implicated in the disease osteoporosis. Here bone mass decreases, becomes fragile, and eventually collapses. This leads to a high frequency of bone breakages and fractures which become increasingly difficult to heal. Osteoporosis is particularly common in middle-aged and elderly women who, after the menopause, produce smaller amounts of the sex hormones that stimulate the formation of new bone. It can be avoided by ensuring sufficient vitamin D and calcium are obtained in earlier life and by taking regular exercise to maintain healthy bone formation.

A study conducted on elderly men living in a home in Boston, Massachusetts, demonstrated the effects of different light sources on the absorption of calcium. The men agreed to be isolated from natural daylight for a period of seven weeks. During this time they remained indoors and under a mixture of typical artificial incandescent light bulbs and fluorescent strip lighting. At the end of the seven week period it was noticed that the men absorbed only forty per cent of the calcium they ingested. Some of the men remained under the artificial lighting for yet another month and their calcium absorption dropped by a further twenty-five per cent.

Another experiment carried out on young healthy men showed that after two months confinement to indoor lighting their vitamin D levels dropped by fifty per cent, and they began to lose more calcium than they were ingesting. In other words, the bones were starting to give up their calcium.

These simple experiments emphasize the degree to which light is essential to the body. They contradict the more recent and popular suggestions that the body should avoid sunshine and its ultra violet rays. In recent years we have been told to keep out of the sun for risk of sunburn, or even skin cancer. Yet we require relatively little sunlight to obtain sufficient ultra violet for vitamin D production: a fair skinned person can generate all the vitamin D required for a day within thirty minutes of exposure to spring or summer light. This is very different from the doses of sun people expose themselves to once or twice a year on their annual two-week holiday. Sunburn is largely an ailment of white skinned industrialized people who, shut indoors all year round, put themselves at risk during their holidays for the sake of an enviable suntan. Alternatively they roast under artificial sunbeds which, while providing the desired skin colouring, can pose a risk of skin damage if overused. The dangers of sunlight are not unfounded, especially for those with fair skin. However, there are ways of obtaining sufficient light for production of vitamin D without burning the skin: regular, short doses of winter, autumn or spring sunlight are rarely dangerous; even summer sunlight if taken in small doses in the early morning or evening rather than during the blistering midday hours is not harmful and will provide the necessary nutrient for calcium metabolism. In addition, a gradual exposure to the sun all year round will provide protection from the summer's harsher rays, and thus prevent burning and the risk of skin cancer during the holidays.

COLOURS OF THE SPECTRUM

But ultra violet is probably not the only component of light which is vital to our health. It is still unclear to what extent other colours of the spectrum affect our biological functioning. Experiments on rats have shown that green light is the most powerful in influencing hormonal function, in particular the suppression of melatonin secretion. The same applies to humans. In an experiment carried out at Jefferson

Medical College in Philadelphia six healthy volunteers were exposed to different coloured light late at night. It was found that blue-green light cut melatonin sharply, while violet and red light actually increased its production slightly. These results have yet to be verified in further experiments. However, if they prove to be correct, the health implications of working under artificial light in its present state could be serious. As we saw in Chapter Two, the levels of melatonin in the blood stimulate or suppress the production of other hormones in the body. For example, melatonin suppresses luteinizing hormone, which in turn suppresses ovulation. Just one of the potential consequences of spending too much time under a light which stimulates the production of melatonin could be infertility.

LIGHT INTENSITY

Colours of the spectrum aside, the most striking difference between sunlight and indoor artificial lighting is intensity. Because of the eye's sensitive and sophisticated mechanism of adapting to different conditions of brightness or dimness, we are often unaware of how dark indoor lighting is in comparison to the natural light outside. It is almost impossible to believe that the light provided by most artificially lit buildings is less than one tenth of that found in the shade on a sunny day outdoors. This means that the total amount of light received by a person working in a conventionally lit indoor environment for sixteen hours a day is considerably less than they would receive in a single hour spent outdoors each day.

Our eyes are well trained to adapt to dim light for visual purposes. However, as we saw in Chapter Three, humans need light of sufficient intensity to regulate their biological clocks. Without it, these subtle daily, monthly and annual rhythms can become disrupted. In the winter, at least, most of us spend a large proportion of our time under static lighting conditions of insufficient intensity to coordinate our body rhythms.

A study carried out in California presented startling evidence of just how little bright light an average human receives in a 24-hour period. A light meter was attached to the wrists of ten healthy subjects to record both the amount and intensity of light received over 24 hours. The results showed that within an average schedule, these people received a very scattered and random distribution of daylight, which rarely exceeded 1,000 lux for more than one hour within the 24-hour period.

If this was the extent of light received in California, one of the sunniest areas of the USA, we may wonder just how little light of sufficient intensity would be received in more northern areas, such as New York, Canada, Britain and Scandinavia.

It is of no surprise therefore, that humans, shut away from natural daylight during the shortened winter days, are showing signs of light deprivation. Vitamin D deficiency is just one indication of the health impact of lack of light. The disturbance of body rhythms – appetite, sleep and mood – is another, as portrayed by a significant number of SAD victims, and an even greater number of sub-syndromal SAD sufferers. Evidence points to the fact that we would all benefit from a greater supply of natural light. But how can this be achieved when most of our waking hours are spent inside under lighting which differs significantly from that of the sun?

One way is to expose ourselves to more natural light by spending more time outside and making adaptations to our indoor environment to encourage in more natural light and light of greater intensity. Chapters Fourteen and Sixteen outline how this can be done.

5

Treatment of the Future

Although the use of bright light to treat SAD is a relatively new discovery, phototherapy is by no means a new phenomenon. The Victorians and Edwardians were often advised to take trips to the mountains or warm European retreats to 'take the air'. Perhaps taking the light was equally vital. Until the Second World War many hospitals were built with verandahs and windows which could be opened up, allowing patients to be wheeled out into the sunshine to help speed their recovery. Even today, oblivious of the reason, perhaps, millions of people from northern climes flee to the light each winter. They go for the warmth, the rest and recreation, but also for the sunlight which relaxes and revitalizes.

In the last ten years treatment with light has become far more specialized than that practised in the early hospitals. Technological advancement has meant we do not have to wheel patients outside for a dose of light, but can give it to them artificially inside. This step forward has come with the development of indoor lighting which replicates the sun's intensity and colour spectrum.

The uses of light in medicine are numerous. As early as 1877 it was discovered that sunlight killed bacteria. Consequently in the early days exposure to its rays was prescribed for diseases as diverse as tuberculosis, cholera, diabetes, gangrene, obesity, chronic gastritis and hysteria. In the mid 1930s Charing Cross Hospital in London used light treatment for diseases of the circulation, such as anaemia, varicose veins and chilblains. Heart disease and digestive disorders were also treated with light. In early operating theatres ultra violet light was even used to clean the atmosphere; it was found that it reduced the number of airborne bacteria by fifty per cent.

LIGHT THERAPY – A POWERFUL MEDICINE

Doctors still use artificial sunlight to treat skin diseases today: herpes and psoriasis are just some of the infections which can be successfully cured with this treatment. In England it was discovered that newborn infants suffering from jaundice showed a slight recovery when their cribs were placed near the window. Today exposure to full spectrum light is standard treatment for jaundiced babies. Although the mechanism by which this cure occurs is unclear, it is thought that phototherapy has a direct effect on the skin which in turn influences the liver, the kidneys and even the blood.

In the previous chapter we saw how lack of sunlight leads to calcium deficiency. The drop in calcium absorption experienced by the men in the Boston home, and the evidence from Leeds showing calcium levels to be at their lowest in winter, emphasize just how important sunlight is to the production of vitamin D, calcium metabolism and the growth of healthy bones. It suggests yet another valuable function for phototherapy today: giving artificial sunlight in controlled doses to the elderly and those who are confined to indoor environments could be of great benefit, particularly during the winter months.

All of these treatments rely on the effects of light on the skin to bring a reaction and cure. But the most recent use of phototherapy in medicine is to direct light through the eyes. This is how doctors over the last ten years have been treating SAD and, more recently, other ailments which are linked to a disruption of the mechanism of natural daylight on the body's hormonal system and biological clocks.

LIGHT TREATMENT FOR SAD

In the early 1980s it was recognized that bright light shining through the eyes of humans brought about changes in hormonal levels in the body. It was also noticed that SAD symptoms of fatigue, depression, over-eating and weight gain were reduced or even cured after four consecutive days of two to four hours phototherapy. Without knowing exactly how light brought these changes, doctors embarked on the successful treatment of many SAD patients. The early SAD clinics of the 1980s used full spectrum lighting of 2,500 lux. In some cases the tubes were fitted into a metal box which was shielded by a plastic diffusing screen. The patients sat in front of these boxes. In other instances the lights were suspended from the ceiling, so that the patient could lie down or move around the room, while still receiving sufficient light.

The light box used to treat SAD should not be confused with a cosmetic sunbed, despite its similarity in appearance. The 'sunlight' provided by sunbeds provides high proportions of ultra violet, the rays necessary to produce a tan quickly. Ultra violet rays are also used in small and highly controlled doses for the skin treatments mentioned above. However, it is the intensity of light in SAD treatment which brings relief, not the specific ultra violet rays. Therefore the bulbs used in the light boxes to treat SAD only contain very small quantities of ultra violet or none at all. They do not radiate sufficient amounts to tan the skin and do not constitute a risk of burning the eyes or body or a risk of skin cancer.

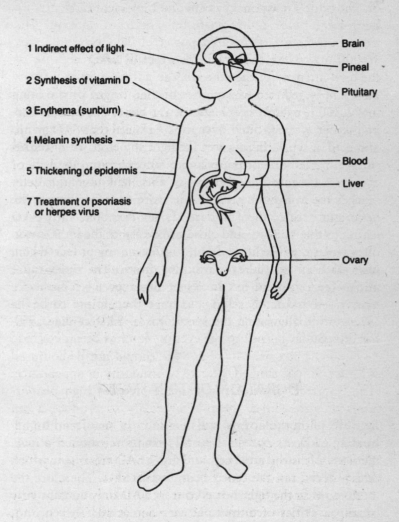

1 Indirect effect of light

2 Synthesis of vitamin D

3 Erythema (sunburn)

4 Melanin synthesis

5 Thickening of epidermis

7 Treatment of psoriasis or herpes virus

Brain

Pineal

Pituitary

Blood

Liver

Ovary

How light affects the different parts of the body, and how it can be used in treatment.

Although most past research on SAD has used full spectrum lighting, it is now known that the required intensity of light for treatment can be met by standard quality fluorescent bulbs rather than full spectrum lighting. The trend in America is to build powerful light boxes of, say, 10,000 lux, using cool white fluorescent tubes. Because of the high intensity of these boxes, the duration of light treatment can be reduced to a quarter of that needed by the original 2,500 lux light box. These newer boxes are designed to be used at a table, tilted over the SAD sufferer who can sit and read or work. In this way the light shines down onto the surface of the book or paper and bounces up into the sufferer's eyes. Despite the intensity of this light box, the light reaches the eye indirectly and therefore does not appear to be brighter than the standard 2,500 lux box. However, owing to the intensity and close proximity of the light, most ultra violet rays are filtered out, to prevent any potential sun burn or harm to the eyes resulting from ultra violet radiation. Ten thousand lux boxes of this type have been extensively tested in the USA and have been found to be as successful in alleviating the symptoms of SAD as the 2,500 lux box. So far no risk to the eyes or skin has been detected.

DURATION OF TREATMENT

Because phototherapy is still a relatively new method of treating SAD, its potential is still being discovered. So new methods of how and when and for how long it should be administered are constantly being explored.

Most research trials carried out in northern and southern hemispheres have required patients to receive between four and six hours of phototherapy per day using a light intensity of 2,500 lux. The treatment was usually split into two parts: one session first thing in the morning and another in the

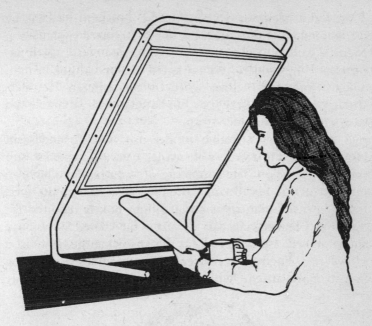

The 10,000 lux overhead light box.

evening. A recovery rate of between seventy-five and eighty per cent was noted in most of these trials within three to four days. The symptoms disappeared as long as the patients continued the treatment. If, however, they stopped phototherapy, the symptoms would return within three or four days.

The duration of phototherapy that each individual requires to relieve SAD symptoms depends on the type of light box used, the severity of the illness and how well the sufferer responds to light. Average light treatment with a 2,500 lux light box is between two and six hours per day. Treatment with the 10,000 lux box is reduced to thirty minutes per day. Because of the inconvenience of spending even a small portion of the day stationary in front of a light box, researchers are now investigating a portable light which can be worn on the head, throwing light forward over the eyes.

This device has been developed and tested in the USA by Dr Rosenthal of the NIMH and Dr Brainard of Jefferson Medical College. The first model comprised two six inch fluorescent lamps which were mounted underneath the brim of a lightweight pith helmet worn by the sufferer. The electronic circuitry and rechargeable battery was contained in a case worn on a shoulder strap.

A more recent portable model uses two incandescent lamps attached to a head visor which can be adjusted to suit the range of vision. The lamps run off a battery and have an intensity of 450 lux. Because the light is so near to the eyes, lower intensity than the standard light box is required for less time. Clinical trials carried out in the United States have shown mixed responses to light therapy using the light visor. However, owing to the convenience it provides in allowing you to move around while receiving light therapy, it may

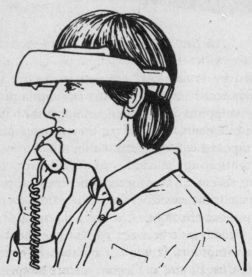

A portable light dosage system worn on the head to allow maximum mobility during treatment.

be worth trying. Some manufacturers operate a rental programme that will allow you to test its efficacy, or a money-back guarantee if it does not provide adequate relief of symptoms.

GETTING THE MOST OUT OF LIGHT TREATMENT

The results of research into the treatment of SAD have proved that the more light sufferers get, the better they feel. However, four or six hours of phototherapy is a heavy commitment and one which not everyone can sustain, although each case is different. Some SAD sufferers need to have at least four hours every day, using a 2,500 lux light box; others find thirty minutes with the same box is sufficient. Some long-term patients have even found that as the winters go by they can whittle down their treatment time without a relapse.

One study carried out in England established that typical SAD cases with clear cut symptoms of depression accompanied by fatigue and drowsiness, food cravings and weight gain tended to have a better response to phototherapy than less typical SAD cases, or cases resembling classical depression (insomnia and decrease in appetite and weight). In this study, patients were given a light box to use at home, thus demonstrating the efficacy of home treatment of SAD.

There is still much controversy over the time of day when therapy is most beneficial. It is generally thought that phototherapy is more effective in the early morning. If this is not possible, midday or evening treatment has also been shown to relieve symptoms. It is not advisable, however, to have treatment after 10 pm, as this can disturb sleep.

Most sufferers generally begin therapy when summer draws to a close. They may start by taking short thirty minute doses of light with a 2,500 lux box, gradually building up the time as the days grow shorter. It is advisable to start therapy before the days grow too short, as some sufferers have noticed that if they wait until the winter is well under way and their symptoms are severe, the treatment is less effective.

There is no doubt that children and adolescents suffer from SAD and can benefit from light treatment just as adults can. However, their condition often differs from that of adult SAD patients. Children generally present milder symptoms and are more sensitive to light therapy, thus requiring fewer hours and less intense lights. Just as children are given milder doses of medicine and drugs, so their dose of light therapy should be shorter. Experiments have shown that children respond well to thirty minutes in front of the 2,500 lux light box in the morning or, if this is not possible, one or two hours in the evening.

SUB-SYNDROMAL TREATMENT

Following the success of phototherapy for SAD, doctors have more recently investigated its use on other people with less severe, but still troublesome, winter symptoms. As we saw in Chapter Two, around twenty-seven per cent of the population are thought to suffer a mild form of SAD, where they experience problematic, but not debilitating symptoms. This is known as sub-syndromal SAD, or S-SAD for short. Studies have been carried out to see if sub-syndromal SAD sufferers could also benefit from phototherapy. The researchers compared the effects of phototherapy on individuals with typical S-SAD winter difficulties, such as low energy, fatigue and appetite increase (see Chapter Two), with others who were aware of seasonal behaviour changes, but did not find them problematic. The results showed that those with distinct S-SAD symptoms responded to treatment: they felt less depressed and tired, and had more energy. The more hours of phototherapy they had, the better they felt. The group with non-troublesome symptoms, however, experienced no change as a result of light therapy. The results of this study imply that those with mild SAD symptoms can also find relief from light therapy in winter, and could perhaps benefit from different lighting conditions in homes and workplaces.

CLASSICAL DEPRESSION

Some psychiatrists are now suggesting that light therapy may be effective in treating non-seasonal, classical depression. Studies have been carried out on groups of depressed patients, offering them bright white light or a placebo, dim red light, as an alternative to anti-depressant medication. Those receiving bright white light responded well to it. In fact, light therapy was seen to be more effective in reducing depression than anti-depressants. Despite the success of these initial trials, more studies are needed before doctors can be sure that phototherapy can be used to treat classical depression and research is still in its early stages.

PREMENSTRUAL SYNDROME (PMS)

Another possible application for phototherapy is in the treatment of PMS. The symptoms of PMS are similar to those of SAD – depression, fatigue, irritability, anxiety, carbohydrate craving, amongst others, and occur in women every month, approximately one or two weeks before the onset of menstruation. So far a small number of women suffering severe symptoms of PMS have been successfully treated with phototherapy. They received two hours of bright light (2,500 lux) daily for one week prior to menstruation, and found that their PMS symptoms were significantly reduced. Further trials are being carried out to establish if light therapy could be a viable treatment for more women suffering PMS.

Regulating Menstruation

Women with irregular periods could also benefit from light therapy. Here the treatment is slightly different from that mentioned above. Women who had irregular periods of between forty-five and sixty days were asked to leave an ordinary 100 watt light bulb on for three days during the 15th, 16th and 17th nights of their cycle. This was found to regularize the timing of their periods and bring the number of days between each period down to between thirty and thirty-two days.

HELPING SHIFT WORKERS

Shift workers who often experience mild depression, fatigue, difficulty with sleeping, and lapses of alertness when working have been offered light treatment to help them adapt to their erratic schedules. Six newsroom workers were given thirty minutes of light of 10,000 lux each evening before setting off for work, and at the same time at weekends. All of the subjects found that light therapy increased their alertness at work, some felt increased energy, and improved sleep, others felt more sociable and better tempered. Further research is being carried out in the USA and the Soviet Union on the use of phototherapy for shift workers.

JET LAG

Several studies have shown how phototherapy can be used to avert jet lag. Experiments carried out by American and

Japanese researchers have shown that travellers flying from west to east experience improved adaptation to local time if they receive two hours of early morning bright light (2,500 lux) for the first three days after their arrival in an eastern location.

The popularity of phototherapy as a successful, non-invasive therapy without significant side-effects has been with us for many years, and, as these examples show, it is likely to be with us for a lot longer. The highly effective use of light therapy in the treatment of SAD has encouraged its use in further applications, to treat other disorders which display themselves on a rhythmical basis and are influenced by quantity or intensity of light, or lack of it. These discoveries will have significant implications for future medicine. They may also usher in a new attitude to how we use lighting in our everyday lives: in schools, hospitals, workplaces, the home, and even perhaps in aeroplanes.

SAD
Winter
Depression

PART
2

6

Understanding SAD

So far we have looked at the reasons for SAD, how it occurs, to whom and why. But how does it really feel and why does it feel the way it does? Although each SAD sufferer's story is different, there are some sensations and experiences that are common to all. This chapter will provide a detailed description of how SAD feels: how the symptoms manifest themselves, why they feel the way they do, and how they can be overcome. Understanding these symptoms and accepting them is one of the first steps towards coping with the syndrome.

DEPRESSION

Of all the SAD symptoms, depression is probably the most debilitating and demoralizing. It leaves sufferers feeling miserable and negative about every aspect of life during the winter months. Suddenly what used to be a fulfilling and meaningful life becomes futile and pleasureless. Apathy sets in, which leads to a chain reaction of guilt, diminished self-confidence and withdrawal.

Nobody knows why depression occurs. In each individual sufferer the onset can result from a wide range of both biological and environmental factors. In the case of SAD it is evidently related to the lack of daylight, but this can be triggered or enforced by a number of other contributing factors, such as early development and childhood experiences, present stresses (the death of a loved one, childbirth, a divorce or work pressure), as well as physical or hormonal disturbances.

Whatever the particular cause or trigger of an attack of depression may be, its result is to create an imbalance in the chemicals of the brain. This in turn disturbs the working of nervous impulses controlling different parts of the body. The most obvious results of such a disturbance are manifested in the areas of thought and behaviour. However, physical symptoms of depression can also occur, even though their importance is usually less severe than that of the psychological symptoms.

Knowing the causes of depression and its effect on the brain is of limited interest to the sufferer. What is of more benefit is knowing the symptoms and being able to recognize them when they strike.

The onset of depression is often insidious. It creeps up and strikes with such a blow that you don't know what has hit you. However, once you have experienced depression, you can, with the aid of the self-help techniques outlined in Part Three, learn to recognize its onset and soften the blow the next time round.

SAD patients have a head start over those suffering from classical depression because they have an approximate idea of when they are likely to start feeling bad. Most diagnosed SAD patients know that as autumn and winter approaches they will feel increasingly depressed. They may also remember that an overcast summer day, or time spent in a badly lit environment can also bring on a bout of misery. Knowing why and when depression might strike allows you to prepare for the onslaught, rather than letting it take you unawares. However, care must be taken not to allow this knowledge to backfire. Some SAD patients have reported that as summer ends they begin to anticipate the depression that they know the autumn will bring. This concern becomes so obsessive that it can even precipitate an early onset of SAD and its associated depression.

It is not enough, therefore, to know when depression is likely to occur, but also to have the knowledge and confidence to deal with it. To do this it helps to be familiar with the type of symptoms you may encounter. Here is a list of the more common feelings experienced with depression.

Psychological

- despair and sadness
- loss of zest for life
- self-negativity and loss of self-esteem
- loss of emotional attachment to friends, family or partners
- feelings of guilt
- tendency to cry
- loss of motivation
- inability to concentrate and memory impairment
- confusion and indecisiveness
- anxiety
- frustration

Physical

- various aches and pains
- muscle weakness
- constipation

One of the principal difficulties facing SAD sufferers is accepting the presence of these symptoms in themselves during the winter months. During the spring and summer SAD sufferers are often highly motivated, successful, energetic and confident personalities. In winter they lose all these qualities. The transformation they undergo is hard to imagine for an outsider, and equally difficult to accept in themselves. Consequently they struggle on, attempting to keep up the same level of activity during the winter months as they achieve in the summer, but failing to do so and becoming miserable, guilty and frustrated in the process. This 'stiff-upper-lip' approach to depression requires much energy to sustain, energy which would be better spent understanding depression and learning to deal with it.

Take Chrystal, for example:

It was the build up to Christmas which was the worst for me. I couldn't concentrate on what to get people for presents. I started feeling panicky, imagining that everyone else had done their Christmas shopping and I hadn't, and thinking I've only got three weeks left, I'll never get my cards written and sent out by then. It was an incredible feeling of not being able to cope. I never thought of saying to myself never mind, it doesn't matter if they don't get their cards. I felt that if I didn't do it I'd be letting myself and everyone else down . . .

I began to dread Christmas, so I tried to simplify the event, but it was impossible, everyone used to come to us. After Christmas I used to hit terrible lows, and I felt desperately depressed, sometimes suicidally depressed, for no reason. I used to wonder why I was depressed, I had everything I wanted, I was so lucky with a lovely husband and family, there was no reason. Everyone else just said: 'you're overtired, there's nothing wrong with you, you're perfectly capable'. And I knew that they were right, normally in the summer I can do half a dozen things at once . . .

One of the reasons why some people refuse to accept depression is because of the stigma attached to mental illness. To be depressed is considered a sign of weakness and inability to cope with life. This theory is unfounded. Although the exact cause of SAD and its subsequent depression is unknown, the link between light and SAD has been established. The onset of the syndrome has nothing to do with weakness or inadequacy, but more to do with external factors such as quantity and intensity of light and its effect on the body. Once this is understood, there should be no reason for SAD sufferers to feel guilty or shameful of their reaction to winter.

For many SAD sufferers, finding relief from depression means accepting that winter puts certain limitations on what they can do and how much they can achieve. Just like Chrystal, most SAD sufferers are very capable during the spring and summer. In the winter they are unable to maintain their self-expectations. Making the transition from summer to winter means modifying goals and expectations so that, instead of feeling guilt and frustration you can sustain a sense of achievement during the winter as well as during the summer. In Part Three a number of practical strategies are suggested which will help in making the transition from summer to winter and alleviate some of the depression caused by doing too much in the winter months.

COGNITIVE THERAPY

Just as rejection of depression consumes energy wastefully, so does the constant search for its source. Instead it is more productive to analyse the thinking patterns and actions which sustain the condition and then follow procedures to change them.

In most cases, asking yourself why you are depressed is futile, because your answer will probably be distorted by your mood. One of the most obvious signs of depression (obvious at least to the outsider, not the sufferer), is an inability to see anything but a negative perception of the world. In this condition rational thinking is impossible.

The theory that depression results from negative ways of viewing the world was pioneered by Dr Aaron Beck who advocated the practice of cognitive therapy. In cognitive therapy people who are depressed are encouraged to alter their distorted negative thinking patterns through reasoning. This therapy has been used with much success in psychiatry and many of the self help suggestions given in Part Three are based on Beck's theories of cognitive therapy. Cognition is the mental process by which knowledge is acquired, hence cognitive therapy is a means of analysing old patterns of thinking and replacing them with new.

According to Beck, one of the first signs of depression is negative thinking. A depressed person begins to place more importance on the negative aspects of his/her experience than on the positive. This results in a tendency to draw general conclusions about the past, present and future of a highly negative nature. As the depression becomes more severe, the sufferer blocks out all positive aspects of present living and focuses exclusively on the negative. Take Melanie, for example:

Melanie is having family problems, the children are being boisterous and disobedient, her husband is unsupportive. She sinks into depression and as her mood gets lower her impression of the situation becomes over-generalized and distorted, both in terms of what is happening, and her own ability to manage the situation in the future. This is what she says:

I'm a complete failure as a mother and a wife, and there's no point in continuing like this because I'm only going to ruin the lives of my children and end up losing my husband.

This is a typical example of a 'cognitive error', or distortion of thinking in depression. Instead of approaching the problem rationally: accepting that the children are being problematic and her husband unresponsive, and in turn considering how the problem could be rationally solved, Melanie jumps to conclusions about her own worthlessness. She blocks out any positive elements which may be present in the situation.

Depressed people tend to make the same cognitive errors again and again. This permits patterns to be recognized and, through the use of therapeutic techniques, corrected. The errors which help sustain depression can thus be averted. The exercises in Chapter Eleven show you how to do this.

Attacking negative thinking is the first means of combatting depression. The second is to encourage a more positive state of mind. It is thought that by engaging in activities which are incompatible with depression – activities which you least feel like doing, like exercise or socializing – negative thoughts become forgotten or minimalized and are unable to be sustained. Getting out and doing things when you feel depressed is not always easy, but is essential in combatting SAD. The self help programme shows how to establish a regular routine of pleasurable activities which will help lift depression and encourage a positive state of mind during the winter months.

CHANGES IN APPETITE AND WEIGHT GAIN

Between sixty-five and seventy-five per cent of SAD sufferers experience an increase in appetite during the autumn and winter. An even greater number find, to their dismay, that their choice of foods changes. Rather than eating balanced meals of proteins, carbohydrates, vegetables and fruit, their preference shifts to a predominance of carbohydrate foods comprising sweets such as chocolate, ice cream, cakes and biscuits, and starches in the form of potatoes, pasta, rice and bread.

On the whole, SAD sufferers eat more carbohydrates than non-SAD people, according to studies carried out in Switzerland, but their desire for starches is particularly enhanced in winter. At this time SAD sufferers also consume more fibre than non-SAD people (fibre also often contains carbohydrate), and they eat more meals, especially in the second half of the day or evening. Coffee and tea intake also increases.

The desire for these foods is strong, yet most sufferers find little pleasure in eating at this time of year. Many crave carbohydrate as a means of gaining energy and warmth or to overcome drowsiness, anxiety and depression. An increase in carbohydrate consumption, coupled with the decrease in activity experienced by almost all SAD sufferers inevitably leads to weight gain. For many an increase of 9lbs (4kg) to 14lbs (7kg) over the winter is not uncommon, although it can be as much as two stone (14kg).

This is how some sufferers experience the change in eating habits:

SALLY

The craving for food would hit me in the evening when I got home from work. I couldn't be bothered to make a meal, so I would work my way through the biscuit tin and then through the bread bin. I'd eat slice after slice of white bread, spreading it thickly with butter and lots of jam or honey. It was like an addiction, I knew while I was doing it that it wasn't doing me any good, but I couldn't stop, it was as if I had to have it.

HELEN

Before light therapy I used to eat more in winter. I easily put on a stone each year. I'd come home and quite happily eat about six doughnuts, something I'd never normally do. Usually one is quite enough. I didn't eat chocolate, but other sweet things, lots of bread and honey and lovely cream and jam doughnuts.

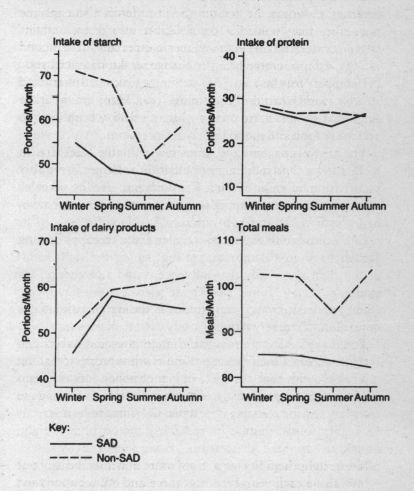

The seasonal variations in eating habits of SAD sufferers, compared with non-SAD controls.

The change in eating habits is not unique to chronic SAD patients. Large numbers of sub-syndromal SAD sufferers have also reported a change in appetite and food preference during the winter months. In fact the general population has a tendency to purchase more starchy food and thus gain more weight in the winter months than in summer.

Why should winter bring a change in appetite and food preference? Why should SAD sufferers seek out sugary and starchy foods when they are feeling low? These are the questions that scientists are now posing in relation both to SAD and other food and mood linked disorders.

The answers to these questions give valuable clues to how SAD sufferers and indeed the population at large can regulate their eating habits in winter. Research has already revealed that the increase in appetite and the craving for carbohydrates in SAD and sub-syndromal SAD sufferers can be regulated to some extent by regular light therapy. Further studies have now demonstrated that eating the right foods at the right times can also influence mood and energy: for example, certain foods can create alertness when you are feeling drowsy, others can induce a feeling of calm when depression or anxiety strikes.

For many SAD sufferers the change in eating habits and weight increases their feeling of guilt and worthlessness. Yet few would say that their craving for carbohydrates stems from hunger or greed. Most would attribute it to a means of releasing tension, anxiety of fatigue. Consumption of starchy or sugary foods, despite its repercussions on body weight, seems to appease depression, anxiety and drowsiness, offering the possibility of a more calm and focused state of mind. This reaction suggests that there is a link between food and mood. What we eat not only affects how our bones and tissues grow and develop, but also influences the functioning of the brain.

WHAT WE EAT AFFECTS OUR MOOD

It is only in the last twenty years that scientists have produced conclusive evidence of the fact that we are what we eat, even in terms of mood and behaviour. Up until the 1970s it was believed that a specialized layer of cells surrounding the brain, known as the blood-brain barrier, separated and insulated it from many of the substances ingested and circulated in the blood. It was considered that regardless of what we ate, and in what quantity, the blood-brain barrier would act as a guard, only allowing certain quantities of certain nutrients into the brain at a given time. However, research carried out since the 1970s has proved that the blood-brain barrier does not impose a limit on the quantity of different nutrients it lets through. This implies that brain chemistry and those aspects of its functioning which are manifested in mood and behaviour are directly linked to what we eat.

In order to understand how this link exists, we need to know a little about how the brain is thought to work, and how thinking and feeling are products of its activity. Nerve impulses are passed through the brain by means of chemical messengers, known as neurotransmitters. Three of these messenger chemicals, dopamine, norepinephrine and serotonin, are manufactured from constituents of the food we eat. Experiments have shown that the function of dopamine and norepinephrine is to stimulate activity in the brain. When levels of these neurotransmitters are high, the brain is able to function more quickly and alertly. Serotonin, on the other hand, has the opposite effect: it eases feelings of stress and tension and allows relaxation. In some people this produces drowsiness, but in others it calms anxiety and agitation and allows concentration.

The three chemical messengers are produced from basic building blocks, or amino acids, found in varying quantities in the food we eat every day. The amount of each building block circulating in the brain determines our mood and levels of activity. In essence, the protein foods we consume, such as meat, fish, pulses, and dairy products, allow more of the activity neurotransmitters (norepinephrine and dopamine) to flood into the brain. In contrast, carbohydrate foods, such as sweets, cakes, bread and potatoes, stimulate the production of brain calming and sedating neurotransmitters, such as serotonin.

This link between the food we eat and mental activity raises the possibility of using food to excite or calm brain activity in much the same way as doctors use drugs. A doctor wishing to arouse a patient suffering from drowsiness might prescribe a drug with a similar effect to dopamine. We now know that it is sometimes possible to achieve the same effect, without drugs, by eating the appropriate foods.

The discovery that the type and quantity of food we eat can influence mood and behaviour is a major breakthrough for people suffering from eating disorders, particularly those which are linked to mood disturbances, as is the case in SAD patients. Scientists are now suggesting that SAD sufferers do not eat starchy, sugary foods out of greed, boredom or despair, but as an inbuilt self help technique: they need the vital nutrients that carbohydrates provide in order to function adequately.

Many SAD sufferers claim that they crave carbohydrates when tense, anxious or mentally fatigued. A packet of biscuits or a few chocolate bars later, they report feeling calmer, more clear-headed and often less depressed. This reaction was studied in an experiment comparing the effects of different food types on two groups of SAD and non-SAD subjects. During the winter months each subject received both a total protein lunch and a total carbohydrate lunch on successive days. Later assessments showed that the two groups showed significant differences in response to the different meals. Carbohydrates appeared to reduce fatigue in

SAD subjects, but increase fatigue in non-SAD subjects. These results tally with the reports by SAD sufferers that they find sweets and starches give them energy.

The mechanism used by our body to determine whether the brain needs protein or carbohydrate is operated by a delicate circuit: as we eat, food passes into the stomach, is processed, and certain nutrients pass into the blood stream and into the brain. When the brain has enough of a certain nutrient it tells us to stop eating. On the whole, the mechanism works pretty well; even when faced with a tempting mound of cream buns or sweet chocolate cake we eventually come to a point where we can eat no more. However, in the case of SAD sufferers some doctors think that this circuit mechanism may be disrupted. As a result the brain fails to respond when carbo-hydrates are eaten and the desire to consume them persists longer than it should. This suggestion was tested out when doctors fed SAD sufferers a serotonin-like drug called d-fenfluramine (not yet on the market) which acts by flooding the brain with serotonin. The effects were dramatic: not only did SAD sufferers stop craving carbohydrates and subse-quently lose weight, they also felt less depressed. Serotonin-active drugs similar to d-fenfluramine are now being used to treat SAD. They are examined in detail in Chapter Nine.

Experiments have also shown that low serotonin levels in the brain bring depression. Other tests have shown that sero-tonin levels in humans are lower in winter than in summer. These facts may account for depression and carbohydrate craving in SAD sufferers and the change in dietary habits found in the population at large during the winter.

Once again, research has hit on a potential cure for SAD, without fully understanding how it works. Why should SAD patients benefit from increased serotonin in winter and how is it that this very different treatment seems to relieve some of the symptoms of SAD, just as light therapy does? The mystery is still to be solved but, in the meantime, SAD patients can profit from the knowledge that their eating habits are not to be blamed on greed or lack of self control, but probably result from an imbalance in the vital chemicals regulating the brain. Armed with this knowledge, sufferers can monitor how different foods affect their mood and energy level and establish an eating programme suited to their winter needs. Chapter Twelve will outline how to do this.

SLEEP

Most people with SAD notice changes in their sleeping patterns during the winter months. The greatest cause for complaint is fatigue and a desire to sleep more. In Britain, seventy-two per cent of SAD sufferers report an increase in sleep time from around seven hours in the summer to nine hours or more in the winter. Doctors call this increase in sleep hypersomnia.

Despite sleeping more, most SAD sufferers do not feel refreshed in the morning. Sleep is restless, and they often wake during the night. The result is that they find it difficult to get up, and feel drowsy throughout the day.

Although they feel tired, a small number of sufferers have problems getting to sleep. They lie awake tossing and turning, and eventually drop off in the early hours of the morning, to wake exhausted.

This is how some SAD sufferers describe their fatigue and sleep symptoms:

MONICA
Throughout the summer I am very busy. I have a large house, three children and we keep horses. I'm often up before six to take the children to gymkhanas. We don't get back till late and then the animals have to be fed, meals prepared and the house organized. I rarely get to bed before midnight.

I started to suffer from SAD about five years ago. I began to notice that I just couldn't keep up my usual routine in winter. For the first time in my life I was unable to get up in the morning when my husband, a farmer, rose at six. Before I had always got up to get his breakfast. I had no energy to do all the jobs which needed doing during the day. I would go upstairs to make the bed around mid-morning and, much to my shame, fall asleep on it. I would take naps, off and on for a few hours in the afternoon, and in the evening, when we sat down to watch television, I nodded off again. My husband went to bed and I would wake up to a buzzing screen. When I did finally get to bed of course I couldn't sleep.

JANE

It's impossible to describe the fatigue SAD brings. At times I was so tired I could only crawl upstairs to bed on my hands and knees. Once I drove all the way to an appointment at the hospital with my head leaning against the window. I didn't even have the strength to hold my head up.

Most of us have periods when we feel the need to sleep more. In fact studies have shown that the population as a whole has a tendency to sleep slightly more in winter than in summer. Sometimes it is difficult to know whether the desire to sleep is a necessity which should be fulfilled, or a whim which should be resisted. Before deciding, it is useful to understand how sleep benefits the body and in what quantities it is most useful.

What is Sleep?

It is generally assumed that long, undisturbed sleep is beneficial. Important work or decisions are often delayed until the morning, in the knowledge that we will feel more refreshed and clear-headed after a good night's sleep. As a result, millions of people each day take sleeping tablets in the hope of getting more or better sleep.

There is more to sleep than the rest it provides. Lying on a bed for two hours does not have the same restorative effect as a one-hour nap. Sleep gives us something more than rest alone, but sleep researchers are still unable to clarify what that is.

Most of us think of sleep as simply a state of non-awakeness, when the brain closes down for the day. Yet doctors have now proved that the brain is highly active while asleep. With the help of a device known as an electro-encephalograph (EEG), which monitors the electrical activity of the brain, recordings can be made of the regular cycles of activity which occur as we sleep.

These recordings have shown that there are different kinds of sleep which we experience in alternating cycles during the night: cycles of quiet and active sleep. During active sleep our brain waves resemble those recorded when we are awake, and our eyes dart beneath closed lids. Active sleep is thus more commonly known as rapid eye movement (REM) sleep. During quiet sleep however, the eyes are more still, this is known as non-rapid eye movement sleep or NREM. This is a time when the brain waves are slow and regular.

During the night there are four or five alternating stages of REM and NREM. As we drop off we start the night with NREM sleep where the brain waves gradually slow down. From this we move into stage two, a slightly heavier sleep, which records twelve or fourteen bursts of brain activity on the ECG. About fifteen to thirty minutes after falling asleep, stages three and four begin. It is now that the brain waves become slower and longer. This is the deepest sleep, said to be the most restful and restorative. It lasts about an hour and then we move back into stage two and almost immediately enter REM sleep. The whole cycle lasts approximately ninety minutes, thus in an eight hour night we may go through four or five cycles. As the night progresses, the periods of deep sleep shorten, while the REM periods grow longer. In fact most of our deep sleep (thought to be the most restorative type) occurs during the first half of the sleep period and constitutes only twenty per cent of total sleep.

Various phases of this normal sleep pattern can be affected by sleep disturbances. For example, the time that elapses before the beginning of the first deep sleep phase can be extended and consequently the first REM phase shortened. Instead of a gradual move into deep sleep, an interval of complete wakefulness might occur, thus shortening the total deep sleep phase and reducing the feeling of rest and restoration in the morning.

Sleep Studies and SAD

Clinical studies have been made on SAD patients, to monitor their sleep and brain wave activity. When compared with non-SAD subjects, it was noted that SAD sufferers showed differences in the type and length of sleep they experience. In the winter months people with SAD sleep longer and experience less deep sleep than non-SAD subjects. Decreased deep sleep, along with frequent disturbances, could be the reason why SAD sufferers awaken unrefreshed and require more sleep during the winter.

Further studies have shown that when SAD patients receive light therapy their sleep patterns change dramatically. Their length of deep sleep increases, and their sleep is less disturbed. Many patients find that their sleep requirements drop by as much as three hours after phototherapy.

How Much Sleep Do We Need?

As we have seen, it is not just quantity of sleep which is important in restoring energy, but the quality and type of sleep. Many of us have the impression that to have 'a good night's rest' we must have at least eight hours of undisturbed sleep. However, just as each of us has different requirements for food and drink, so each of us is exceptional in the number of hours of sleep required to feel rested. Napoleon I, for example, and Edison, the inventor of the light bulb, were able to achieve feats of great intellect and physical endurance, on between two and four hour's sleep a night. They were what is known as short sleepers. Einstein, on the other hand, was a long sleeper, and functioned better on more sleep. The range of sleep required in most adults can deviate from as little as four hours to fourteen, depending on our age, lifestyle and, of course, the time of year.

For this reason, it is essential for anyone who suffers sleep problems, be it too much or too little sleep, to establish approximately how many hours he/she really requires. For SAD sufferers this will differ according to the time of year. Chapter Thirteen of the self-help SAD programme will explain how to assess sleeping requirements, and indicate ways of adhering to the sleep time allocated. It will also suggest ways of adapting your lifestyle to your winter sleep requirements, and give tips on how to gain the most from sleep during this season, in order to boost energy and alleviate feelings of fatigue and lethargy during the day.

SPRING MANIA

Much research has been carried out to explore how and why depression occurs in SAD sufferers. Less has been written about the dramatic and sometimes problematic mood swing many experience at the end of winter. Between seventy and ninety per cent of SAD patients experience a surge in mental and physical energy when the days lengthen. This feeling contrasts dramatically with the torpor and fatigue felt during the winter. In spring confidence returns, along with heightened energy, sexual appetite and a reduced desire to eat and sleep.

In many cases this change of mood is welcome. When it is a mild reaction it is termed hyperthymia and it simply brings energy levels back to normal and provides an increased sense of well being. Depression is lifted, weight is shed and the sufferer can get on with life as normal. However, in some cases, this so-called spring fever is more than an elated mood, it turns to what is known as hypomania, a state of hyperactivity characterized by increased energy, enthusiasm and confidence which leads to impatience and irritability with colleagues and family. Hypomanics have a tendency to talk and act irrationally, they seek greater excitement in life and start to perceive things differently from those around them. Inability to sleep, feelings of extravagance and excessive spending are common signs of hypomania.

More serious still than hypomania is true mania, found in fifteen to twenty per cent of SAD sufferers. Manic patients cannot sleep, their increase in energy is such that they stay awake all night. If left untreated, mania can lead to total and life-threatening exhaustion. Sufferers tend to talk rapidly and sometimes incoherently, and their thoughts are racy and distracted. Their increased self-confidence turns to grandiose and unreal self illusions and ambitions which can sometimes lead to impractical professional decisions and extravagant financial actions. Heightened sexual energy often leads them to embarrassing and unexpected promiscuity.

Doctors refer to SAD patients as either unipolar or bipolar. In unipolar patients, mood simply goes down in winter; they become depressed, but in spring their mood returns to normal. They do not experience any of the adverse spring symptoms mentioned above. Bipolar patients, on the other hand, move between the two extremes of depression and mania. Their mood goes right down in winter and comes

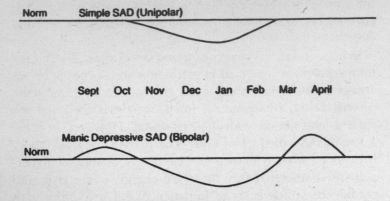

Different SAD personalities (northern hemisphere).

right up in spring or summer. People who suffer true mania are said to be bipolar I. People with the less severe, but still problematic hypomania are said to be bipolar II.

Mood swings of the type found in bipolar depression are also diagnosed in people who suffer classical affective disorder, also known as manic depression. However, in classic manic depression the mood swings can occur at any time, unlike bipolar SAD, which generally brings two regular, major mood swings per year, which coincide with the transition from summer to winter and winter to spring.

Summer mania is not a new phenomenon, it was noticed long before SAD was recognized as a treatable syndrome. Cases crop up throughout the history of medicine, and constant references are made to its relationship with the seasons. The earliest recording is in seventeenth century England, where an English noblewoman was noted to have suffered regularly recurring winter depressions and summer manias. Her doctor, noted that 'there are twin symptoms, which are her constant companions, mania and melancholy, and they succeed each other in a double and alternate act . . .'

Bipolar illness was first clearly defined by Emil Kraepelin, a

German psychiatrist who practised at the beginning of this century. Kraepelin described patients with recurrent winter depression and summer mania, and wrote that he:

> repeatedly . . . saw in these cases moodiness set in in autumn and pass over in spring when the sap shoots in the trees, to excitement, corresponding in a certain sense to the emotional changes which come over even healthy individuals at the changes of the seasons. (Kraepelin, E. (1921) *Manic Depressive Insanity and Paranoia*, G. Robertson (ed), R. Barclay (trans), (Edinburgh: E. & S. Livingstone).

Kraepelin here suggests that the change in mood which comes in the spring is felt by everyone. By this he implies that SAD and its characteristic spring mania lies at the end of a spectrum of graded seasonal behaviour experienced by all of us.

A number of successful and famous individuals have been noted to fall within this spectrum of seasonal mood swings. Winston Churchill is said to have suffered from serious prolonged bouts of depression. Although he was not a SAD sufferer, he is said to have experienced mood swings, alternating from depression to intense activity, suggestive of hypomania. During his periods of energy Churchill was forceful, striving and tireless, and could manage a number of different tasks at once, combining his brilliant skills as a politician with his ability to organize the war cabinet, while also producing a vast amount of written material. He had an enormous capacity for work, much of which was carried out during the night hours. In his early political career his bouts of grandiose ideas and sometimes reckless behaviour, typical of hypomania, evoked suspicion and fear in some of his contemporaries, who tried in vain to keep him in check. These highs were interspersed with depressed periods which Churchill referred to as his 'black dog', when he refused to venture out and his thoughts turned to despair, and even suicide. During his later years as prime minister he appears to have had greater control of his moods and put his extensive energy into the war effort. But even in his old age he continued to work through the night, exhausting his younger colleagues.

Just as Churchill used his mood swings to his advantage, and that of the country, so many sufferers of bipolar SAD find they can profit from their springtime high to make up for time lost in the winter. The first SAD patient diagnosed at the National Institute of Mental Health, Herb (see Chapter Two) kept diaries of his activity and mood during the thirteen years before he was diagnosed and treated. He noted that during his depression he experienced a dramatic fall in work activities: he attended fewer meetings and even made fewer telephone calls. When in mid-winter his period of hypomania started, he began to look forward to going to work, his creativity returned and his previously sluggish thoughts started to race. His energy level increased and he needed far less sleep. By March he notes that he was able to function

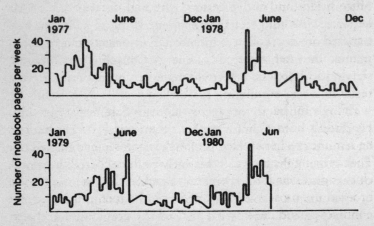

The numbers of notebook pages Herb wrote per week fluctuated with the seasons, as this graph shows.

happily on only two or three hours a night. Herb plotted his activities on a graph, which showed his annual peaks and troughs of activity.

Herb was fortunate in that he was aware of his mood swings; his high energy in the spring and the creativity it brought allowed him to make up for his inactivity in the winter. Although this was not an ideal way to exist, at least it allowed him to continue working.

Other SAD sufferers are less aware of the mood swing which occurs in bipolar SAD. The sudden increase in energy takes over so rapidly that it can get them into difficult and sometimes embarrassing situations. Take Penny for example:

Penny had spent the winter feeling depressed, tearful and antisocial. Although she worked part time, she had taken many days off sick because she just couldn't face going to work. Around the middle of March she started to perk up. One weekend she spent the whole two days clearing out cupboards and spring-cleaning, and reproaching her husband and sons for letting the place get in such a mess. She was at the office bright and early the next day and quickly completed her work. Although she was pleased to feel better, she was irritated by her colleagues' lack of enthusiasm and disappointed that her work offered no challenge. To compensate she decided to call a few friends and arrange to meet up in a restaurant that evening.

Penny's husband, George, was pleased at her suggestion. He hadn't been able to get her to go out for months. But he felt uneasy, her sudden transformation seemed unnatural. That evening Penny was excitable, she dressed in flamboyant clothes and was loud and extravagant in the restaurant. She ordered the most expensive items on the menu, but scarcely a morsel passed her lips. He noticed she drank a lot and also ordered after dinner liqueurs, which normally she didn't touch. During the meal Penny was very animated, she kept the conversation going, and added some indiscreet jokes and witticisms which finally led to her making a few suggestive comments to one of their male friends, causing embarrassment to the whole party.

On their way home George reproached Penny for her comments at the dinner table. She flared up, quick to reply that he was becoming staid and boring. She claimed that she was fed up with being 'a good little housewife', she wanted a career and excitement, she even mentioned the thought of having a fling with another man. It was past midnight when they got home. George went to bed, hurt, but Penny stayed up listening to music downstairs. George's reproach had annoyed her; hadn't she been the life and soul of the evening? She eventually went to bed at two, having decided that she would approach her boss the next day for a better position and a raise in salary.

Of course Penny's boss was somewhat surprised by the sudden transformation which had taken place. Although Penny put up a forceful and convincing argument for promotion, her boss reminded her of the fact that she had often taken time off sick during the winter, and more than once had complained that her work load was too great. A heated discussion followed, where Penny criticized her boss's method of handling employees and flounced out of the office. Feeling angry and tearful she headed to the centre of town, where she appeased her anger by splashing out on £300 worth of clothes. She also ordered a new washer dryer. All of this was paid for by credit card.

When George got home that evening and heard Penny's account of the day he was worried. He found her highly excited and emotional and, much to her anger, he decided to call his local doctor for some advice.

Penny was suffering from acute hypomania but, unlike Herb, she did not recognize her change in mood from winter to spring. Had she been more aware of her sudden surge in energy, she could have channelled it into more positive acts and avoided some of the embarrassment, expense and confrontation caused.

For many years doctors have been looking for the cause of mania. Its link with the seasons has been noted over the centuries. Studies of hospital admission records in many parts of the world show that the highest number of admissions to hospitals of people suffering from mania occurs during the spring, summer or autumn. Winter has the fewest admissions.

Originally, doctors attributed the onset of spring and summer mania to the rise in temperature. In the early asylums treatment consisted of plunging manic patients into ice cold baths! More recent research over the last eight years has shown that it is not the temperature which precipitates mania, but the increase in day length and hours of sunshine that occurs in spring and early summer. In a study carried out at the University Psychiatric Department of Galway in Ireland over five years, it was noticed that admission rates for mania correlated significantly with monthly hours of sunshine and daylength, but showed no significant relationship to variations in temperature, rainfall or atmospheric pressure.

Doctors investigating SAD suggest that spring fever, hypomania and mania may be an abnormal response to light. Their research has shown that people with mania show a greater drop in night melatonin levels on exposure to bright light than non-manic patients. Perhaps bipolar SAD sufferers are more sensitive to light than others.

The link between mania and the seasons is well established. Research is continuing in the hopes of finding which aspects of the seasons bring about this change, and why some SAD sufferers experience hypomania or mania and others don't. Why mania occurs is of less importance than knowing when and how it occurs. Learning to anticipate the onset of hypomania or mania is important to SAD sufferers because it allows them to better control its effects. Being aware of the onset of hypomania or mania will greatly help in preventing its embarrassing and sometimes dangerous consequences.

Chapter Fourteen, part of the self help SAD programme, tells you how to monitor your moods and develop an awareness of any sudden changes which may occur in spring. It indicates how you can avoid the reckless behaviour which sometimes results from hypomania and instead use these changes positively. People who live with or are near to SAD sufferers can help in this. Advice on how to spot symptoms of mania in others and what to do about it are given in Chapter Seventeen.

Self Help
SAD
Programme

═══════════

PART
3

═══════════

7

Self Diagnosis

In the previous chapters we looked at the theory behind SAD: what it is, who suffers and why. We now look at how to treat the syndrome with the aid of a total self help SAD programme.

First you will be asked to complete a detailed self-diagnosis questionnaire which will tell you if you are a SAD sufferer and, if so, how badly you suffer – chronic SAD, sub-syndromal SAD or mild winter blues. On the strength of this diagnosis you can then decide on the best treatment. Most people find that light therapy provides the most effective and rapid relief from the symptoms of SAD or sub-syndromal SAD. To complement light therapy the following chapters offer a number of self help techniques which, by combatting the individual symptoms one by one, give further impact to your all-round winter programme.

The self help SAD programme advises how to go about getting light therapy, how to incorporate it into your life, and how to use it to your best advantage. It outlines other possible treatments for SAD, which can be used either as alternatives, or together with light therapy. These treatments are particularly useful to those with milder winter symptoms, who do not necessarily require light therapy. The programme gives self help exercises to combat symptoms of depression and fatigue and others which will boost energy. It offers an eating plan which, without depriving you of your favourite winter foods, will help control carbohydrate craving and keep winter weight gain to a minimum. It suggests an outdoor programme which will provide you with fresh air, natural light and exercise, all essential in combatting SAD. Finally, it suggests simple techniques which allow you to transform your home into a spring haven. Used together, these different techniques offer an all-round concerted assault on the symptoms of SAD.

ARE YOU SAD?

Before embarking on a self help programme, it is important to first establish if you are suffering from SAD and how seriously. Below is a questionnaire which will allow you to make a self diagnosis of your condition in winter. It is based on the diagnostic criteria designed by Dr Rosenthal at the National Institute for Mental Health, USA, and is used by Professor Thompson in SAD clinics in Britain, and by other doctors and psychiatrists all round the world. Your response to this questionnaire will indicate if you suffer from SAD, be it in its acute form or at the milder sub-syndromal level. Once your condition has been established you can, if appropriate, proceed to the self help programme outlined in the rest of this section.

SAD QUESTIONNAIRE

Before answering this questionnaire it is important to establish your geographical location over the last three years. Your reaction to winter will depend to some extent on where you live, and may be influenced by a move to an area nearer or further from the equator. If you have lived in the same area for the last three years, go on to complete the questionnaire. If you have moved to an area which is significantly further north or south than your previous location, stop a moment to consider if your reaction to winter has changed since the move. Do you find it easier to cope with winter, or more difficult? Note down your thoughts, and then go on to complete the questionnaire.

Part A

Think back over the last three years and recall the time of year at which you generally feel your worst (If you are in the northern hemisphere choose answers from section I, if you are in the southern hemisphere, choose from section II):

I (NORTHERN HEMISPHERE READERS)
   a December, January and February
   b May, June and July
   c I feel bad all year round
   d I don't feel bad at any particular time of year

II (SOUTHERN HEMISPHERE READERS)
   a June, July and August
   b December, January and February
   c I feel bad all year round
   d I don't feel bad at any particular time of year

If your answer to Part A was a, it is likely you are suffering from a winter disorder of some degree. To discover how serious it is, continue to Part B.

If your answer to Part A was b or c it is possible that you are suffering classical depression or an unusual type of SAD which afflicts a very small minority of people in the summer months, rather than the winter. If either of these conditions affects you badly enough to disrupt your lifestyle: if it jeopardizes your job, relationship with friends, spouse or family, or makes you too unhappy to function properly, you should consult your doctor or a nearby psychiatric clinic.

Part B

Look at the table on the opposite page. To what degree do the items in the left-hand column change with the winter? (Place a tick under the heading which seems most appropriate.)

HOW TO SCORE:

Calculate the value of your ticks according to the box in which they were placed.

None   = 0
slight   = 1
moderate = 2
marked   = 3
extreme   = 4

Now add up your total score. You may have anything between 0 and 24.

- If you scored between 0–7 you show signs of winter changes, but you are fortunate that they do not affect your overall well being and functioning.
- If you scored between 8–11 the winter changes you experience are quite noticeable, and could be problematic. You are likely to be suffering from sub-syndromal SAD, and would certainly benefit from following the self help programme. Depending on the severity of your ailments, you could benefit from light therapy, though it may not be essential.
- If you scored 11 or more, winter changes constitute a problem which affects your daily life and functioning. With this score it is likely you are suffering from SAD. In your case there is a high chance that light therapy will relieve many of your symptoms and you will certainly benefit from the self help programme.

Now look at the chart again. Consider if your answers would have been the same last year. What about the year before? Doctors usually make a diagnosis of SAD if their patient has had three winters of SAD, two of which are

	NONE	SLIGHT	MODERATE	MARKED	EXTREME
SLEEP LENGTH					
SOCIAL ACTIVITY (consider meetings with friends, parties, dinners, Christmas)					
MOOD (consider your feelings about yourself and your life)					
APPETITE (consider quantity and type of food)					
WEIGHT GAIN		(0-2lbs)	(2-5lbs)	(5-9lbs)	(9lbs+)
ENERGY LEVEL					

consecutive. If you have a high SAD score and you remember having two other consecutive winters where you felt the same, you are likely to be a SAD sufferer.

It may be that you find yourself on the border-line of one of the three categories mentioned above. In the case proceed to Part C of this questionnaire, which will help to clarify the severity of your symptoms. You may give as many answers as you like to these questions, or none at all, according to how appropriate they seem to your condition.

Part C

1 IF YOU TAKE A WINTER HOLIDAY IN THE SUN (WINTER SPORTS INCLUDED) DOES IT
    a help you get through the rest of the season without noticeable problems?
    b make no difference to your general mood?
    c improve your mood, but when you return home again you quickly become depressed again?

2 AS FAR AS YOUR SEX LIFE IS CONCERNED
    a do you regularly lose interest in the autumn/winter?
    b do you resume interest in the spring?
    c you aren't ever interested?
    d the seasons make no difference?

3 IN YOUR FAMILY IS THERE
    a a history of alcoholism?
    b a history of winter depression?
    c a history of classical depression?
    d none of these?

Your SAD score will go up if you gave the following answers to part C:

1 a or c
2 a or b
3 a, b or c

your SAD score will be pushed down if you answered:

1 b
2 c
3 d

You should now be in a position to judge to what extent winter affects you. Are you one of the five to ten per cent of SAD sufferers? Or do you fall into the larger sub-syndromal category? Perhaps you are lucky enough not to suffer from SAD at all. If, however, you recognise a definite winter pattern of symptoms, however mild, the following self help programme will help you overcome them. Winter does not have to be a time of low productivity, misery and frustration. Read on to find out how you can combat SAD.

8

Light Therapy

Bright artificial light has been used increasingly over the last decade to treat SAD and sub-syndromal SAD. In research trials all over the world it has proved to be a powerful means of relieving, and even removing SAD symptoms, without causing any significant side-effects.

Between seventy-five and eighty per cent of sufferers find that light therapy considerably alleviates depression. After a few days' treatment they feel less depressed and more energized. At night they sleep better and awake refreshed. Because light therapy reduces the desire to nibble or binge on carbohydrate, appetite and weight gain are also reduced. The therapy is carried out using a specially designed box which produces a light intensity of at least 2,500 lux. It is an ideal therapy for self help, home use, providing it is used correctly and on a regular basis.

This chapter explains all you need to know about light treatment. It outlines how to obtain it, either at a clinic or at home, and how to choose a light box which most suits your needs. Most important of all it helps you to establish a routine which allows you to incorporate light therapy into your life with the minimum disruption and the maximum benefit.

HOW TO GET LIGHT THERAPY

There are two ways of obtaining light therapy. One is to apply to a SAD clinic which offers treatment under medical supervision. The other is to make your own diagnosis, buy your own equipment and carry out the treatment at home.

CLINICAL RESEARCH

The resource section at the back of this book has a list of SAD clinics. Most of them carry out research into SAD and light therapy and are keen to find SAD sufferers to participate. If there is a research project being carried out near your home this would be an excellent way to obtain therapy and learn about your illness. You can write to the person carrying out the research, or telephone and make enquiries. Explain that you think you are suffering from SAD and ask for more information about the research and treatment. Give a name and address where you can be contacted, along with a home telephone number.

You may be sent a questionnaire to fill in. If you apply in the summer, you may be asked to wait until the autumn or winter, when your symptoms start. You will then have an appointment with a psychiatrist who will make a diagnosis to see if you are suffering from SAD, and consider if light therapy could help you.

Before manufacturers started making light boxes commercially, the only way to obtain light therapy was to take part in medical research. The first people to be successfully treated for SAD underwent supervised light therapy in psychiatric institutions. Although many of them disliked the idea of participating in 'experiments' at first, they soon realized that it was an interesting and fulfilling experience: they learnt a great deal about their illness, met other fellow sufferers and found a highly effective treatment. Moreover, they felt they were contributing to discoveries which would benefit others in the future.

The great advantage of receiving treatment from a SAD clinic is the reassurance of being closely monitored by medical professionals. This is most important if you are taking antidepressant drugs or tranquillizers.

If you do not want to contact the clinic directly yourself, try consulting your doctor. Because SAD is still relatively new, he/she may not be aware of the illness, although it has been reported extensively in medical journals in Europe, Canada, Australia, New Zealand and the USA. Most doctors are keen to try anything which may assist in solving a problem, but if your doctor seems unwilling to write to the SAD clinic on your behalf do not be put off, you can still apply yourself.

If you live too far away from a SAD clinic, or do not wish to have supervised treatment, you are now equipped with a self-diagnosis questionnaire and a self help programme. The resources section at the back of the book also gives a list of light box manufacturers. The rest of this chapter will tell you how to safely and efficiently go about home treatment.

BUYING A LIGHT BOX

There are many different light boxes on the market. The one you buy will depend ultimately on your needs and lifestyle and how you plan to incorporate light therapy into your day. You should also consider the extent to which the box has been tested and over what period of time it has been used. When purchasing a light box you should bear these points in mind:

- WHAT KIND OF LAMPS ARE PROVIDED; FULL SPECTRUM OR FLUORESCENT?
  Early research into the treatment of SAD used full

spectrum bulbs which produce a light that closely approximates natural daylight. However, more recent research has revealed that high-intensity fluorescent bulbs are equally effective, and do not contain the harmful ultra violet rays contained in daylight and full-spectrum lighting. Most manufacturers today use filters to remove ultra violet rays. Be sure that any light box you use has an ultra violet reducing mechanism.

- IS SUFFICIENT INTENSITY (LUX) EMITTED?
  The light box should produce at least 2,500 lux when you are seated three feet away from it.
- ARE THE BULBS PROTECTED BY A SCREEN?
  The screen is important, as it absorbs high energy radiation.
- HAS THE UNIT BEEN ADEQUATELY TESTED IN CLINICAL TRIALS AND, IF SO, HAVE THESE TRIALS BEEN DOCUMENTED?
  Try to get hold of any such documentation before you buy.
- STYLE: STANDARD, PORTABLE OR WINDOW BOX?
  The original light box is a metal case containing eight 24 inch (96cm) tubes. This is placed on the floor or a table three feet from where you are sitting so that the light is at eye level. More recent models are now made in such a way that they can be folded, suitcase fashion, and carried about. If you need to transport your box regularly, this is a good choice. There is also a fluorescent model, which is designed to resemble a window.
- HIGH OR LOW INTENSITY?
  The 2,500 lux full spectrum light box has been used most widely in research over the last ten years. The 10,000 lux fluorescent box has been used in trials over the last five years and is growing in popularity. Extensive tests have been carried out on both models and neither have shown adverse side-effects.

When considering which box to buy think of the time you have available for light therapy. What is your schedule? You will need to use the low intensity box for between two to six hours per day; the high intensity box has the same effect with only thirty minutes treatment per day.

Some SAD clinics allow patients to borrow light boxes on a trial basis. Some light box manufacturers are prepared to let you return the box if you find it does not help relieve your symptoms. If possible it is advisable to wait until your symptoms start and try a box before making the investment.

Light fixtures cannot be prescribed on the National Health Service in Britain, but they have been recognized as medical equipment, and can thus be purchased free of VAT. In the United States, some insurance companies have been known to reimburse the cost of phototherapy equipment. The best way to obtain reimbursement for a light box is by asking your doctor to write a letter explaining your condition and substantiating your claim.

HOW TO USE THE LIGHT BOX

Once you have chosen a light box suited to your needs and schedule, it is essential to know how to use it correctly. The objective is to allow as much light as possible to enter the eye. Wearing spectacles should not inhibit the effects of treatment, providing the lenses are not too thick. Contact lenses can also be retained, although it is recommended that you remove them during the treatment if they become a source of irritation.

Upright Box/Portable or Non-portable (2,500 or 10,000 lux)

Position yourself or the box so that the light is at eye level. You can place the box on a table or desk where you can sit in front of it, or on the floor, providing you are seated low enough to receive the light. You should be within three feet of the box for

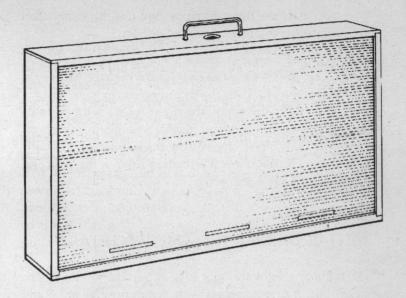

The window light box.

the light to naturally filter into your eyes. It is not necessary to stare at the bulbs, you can read, watch television or carry out some other task. You should not sleep however, but try to glance at the light every thirty seconds or so.

Tilted Box (10,000 lux)

This box is designed to be used at a desk or table at which you must be seated with your legs underneath. The light will be over and above you, so you do not need to glance up at it, but can concentrate on reading or writing, looking down at the surface of the table. Take care not to lean over your work and cast a shadow over your page, thus blocking the light your eyes receive.

Dawn Simulator

The Natural Alarm Clock dawn simulator is a convenient form of light treatment. It looks like a bedside light with a built-in clock. You set the time you want to wake just as on any normal alarm clock. In the morning, starting 30 minutes before your wake-up time, the light starts with a faint glimmer, then gets brighter and brighter, simulating a natural sunrise. The body clock receives the missing signal and with less disruption to the natural circadian rhythm the user can feel more positive and energetic.

ESTABLISHING A TREATMENT SCHEDULE

When beginning light therapy it is important to make sure you get enough to counteract your symptoms. Most people

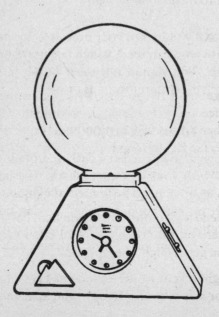

need at least two hours using the 2,500 lux box or thirty minutes using the 10,000 lux box.

Think of light therapy as you would your personal hygiene, your daily meals, or your sleep. It is something you need to do every day, so decide on a regular time which will be set aside for this purpose. Most people find that early morning light is the most effective, but if this is not convenient, the therapy will also be effective at other times of the day. However, avoid treatment after 10 o'clock at night as this may disturb your sleep.

Remaining stationary in front of a light box for two hours everyday is not an easy feat. You will find that it is easier to incorporate into your lifestyle if you choose a regular time to do it, and decide how you will occupy yourself during this time. You may decide that this is a welcome opportunity to relax and do nothing. Alternatively you could use the time to read, listen to the radio, or watch television.

Here are some examples of how SAD sufferers incorporate light therapy into their routine:

'I keep the light box by my bed. When my husband wakes up he switches the light box on, then brings me a cup of tea, so I can gently wake up basking in the light.'

'I generally get up early, go down and make myself breakfast and coffee and take it into the room where I have my light box. Then armed with a good book I sit in front of the box; it makes me feel so relaxed.'

'I usually time my therapy to watch a favourite television programme, or listen to something on the radio.'

'Because I spend a lot of time in the kitchen, I often have the light box there on the work top. As I chop vegetables or wash up I can get my light therapy too.'

'I keep my light box at work. As soon as I get into the office it goes on for a few hours. Then in the afternoon, when I feel drowsy I often flip it on to perk me up. My colleagues are quite intrigued, some even envious, that I've got something they haven't.'

'I have a trolley I can wheel the box around on. Because I have small children, I find it hard to sit still for two hours at a stretch, so I try to keep it on most of the time, moving it around with me. Ideally I would have a box in every room!'

'I usually have one hour in the morning, and one in the early evening, sometimes during the day if I sit down for a cup of tea or coffee, I put it on to give me a boost.'

The time of year you start therapy depends on you, your location and what the weather is like. Experienced SAD sufferers start gradually with phototherapy when summer draws to a close. They may begin by taking short thirty minute doses of light with a 2,500 lux box, gradually building up the time as the days grow shorter. Wait for your symptoms to appear, but do not put off treatment for too long, as this may hold up your recovery.

Monitor the effect light therapy has on you. After five days of treatment you will probably find that you are feeling better. However tempting it may be, don't stop the therapy as you will find after three or four days without it the symptoms return with a vengeance. If you find no relief after five days increase your therapy time to three hours for the next four days. If there is still no response, try four hours treatment per day for four more days. If you still have no response it is unlikely light therapy will help you. At this point you should turn to some of the other treatments outlined in this book in Chapters Nine and Ten.

It is possible that you will experience an initial improvement after starting light therapy followed by a lull during which your symptoms return. The reason for this may be that part of your improvement was due to the placebo effect (see

Chapter Two), where your mind imagines you are getting better. Sometimes it is difficult to assess whether light therapy has really made an improvement. You may underestimate the change which has taken place, or alternatively be over-optimistic. If you are in doubt, ask someone if they have noticed a change in you: are you more productive, outgoing and cheerful?

Through trial and error you will know how much light therapy you need and when. January and February are thought to be the worst months for SAD suffers in the northern hemisphere, July and August in the southern hemisphere, so treatment should be at its peak duration during this time. After these months you can try to reduce the time slightly, but wait until around mid-April (northern hemisphere), or mid-October (southern hemisphere) to put away the lights altogether.

Even though the official months for SAD suffering are the winter months, overcast days in spring or summer may bring a relapse of symptoms. If this is the case do not hesitate to use the light box to give yourself a booster and compensate for the grey, gloomy days.

LIGHT THERAPY FOR CHILDREN

There is no doubt that children and adolescents suffer from SAD (see Chapter Two) and can benefit from light treatment just as adults can. However, their condition often differs from that of adult SAD patients. Children generally present milder symptoms and are more sensitive to light therapy, thus requiring fewer hours and less intense lights. Experiments have shown that children respond well to thirty minutes in front of the 2,500 lux light box in the morning or, if this is not possible one or two hours in the evening. Try to incorporate light therapy into a child's life without too much fuss.

Children hate to be different from their contemporaries. Have the box on while the child is getting up and dressing, or put it on during a television programme. Older children could have it on a desk while doing homework or reading.

SIDE EFFECTS

Between seventy-five and eighty per cent of people suffering from SAD or sub-syndromal SAD feel better after three or four days of consistent light therapy. Some feel an immediate improvement after the first dose, others take several days to respond. Even after as little as twenty minutes' exposure, some sufferers report a sense of calm as their muscles relax and their attention is more focused.

Some sufferers have reported mild side-effects from light treatment. These are not dangerous and, compared with some of the unpleasant side-effects of anti-depressant drugs, are minimal. Moreover, the side-effects of light therapy are usually temporary, and can generally be remedied by reducing exposure time.

Some of the most common initial side-effects of light therapy are headaches, eye irritation (itching or stinging), and slight nausea. Usually these effects subside a few hours after treatment is finished. They generally disappear altogether after several exposures. Unless you are in extreme discomfort it is worth putting up with minor irritations for a few days, until you adapt to the light. If, after four days, the irritation persists or becomes worse, sit a little further away from the light box, reduce your exposure, and consult a professional trained to treat SAD.

You may experience a surge in energy after light treatment which makes you irritable and hyperactive. Gradually reduce the dosage if this happens until you find your optimum requirement.

It is possible that you may become depressed during a cold or viral infection. Light therapy could at this time cause irritation. However, soon after the infection or virus has cleared up, the positive effects of the light will return.

WHEN NOT TO USE LIGHT THERAPY

There are very few cases when light therapy should not be used. However, if you have an eye or skin condition which is affected by bright light you should consult a doctor before embarking on light therapy. The bright light could emphasize an eye problem or cause a rash in a skin condition. If you suffer from hypertension, diabetes or have any history of eye disease in the family it is advisable to seek medical advice before starting light therapy. Most people find that light therapy is a highly effective treatment which has no adverse repercussions. Here are some case histories:

JENNIFER

I first investigated light therapy in 1986 after six winters of depression. After my initial enquiry at the clinic I completed a questionnaire and was seen immediately. It was agreed that I should return as soon as my depression began in the autumn.

I saw Professor Thompson in October 1986 and we agreed that I should try light therapy. We decided that it would be sensible to gradually reduce the drugs I was taking (lithium carbonate to control mood swings and anti-depressants) to be able to assess the effectiveness of light therapy. This took three weeks and, although I became very depressed, I felt much more positive than I had for some time: I felt secure, because I was very well looked after, and hopeful, because there was a good chance that I could get better.

By the fourth week I was ready to test the light therapy. I went into hospital on Monday and, on Tuesday and Wednesday nights, received light therapy of different intensities along with another woman. During the therapy we had regular blood tests to assess the physiological changes induced by light therapy. Odd though it may seem, I enjoyed it enormously. Being in a research ward and participating in a project which could help me and eventually many others was totally different from my previous hospital experiences, which filled me with dread. At Charing Cross the staff were unfailingly tolerant and courteous with me, even when I was being unpleasant and uncooperative. This attitude was extended to all the patients in the psychiatric unit whether or not they were helping with research.

On Thursday I went home to start testing the lights over a period of six weeks as an out-patient. I was given one of the hospital's light boxes to use and, for the first week used it for two hours everyday. Within four days of this treatment, the improvement was almost miraculous. My mood and energy levels soared to a peak not experienced for many years (during the winter at least), and I immediately applied for and got a new job and started contacting family and friends.

The aim of the research at this time was to see how much light was needed to alleviate symptoms of SAD and how effective the treatment was. During the trial I went to Charing Cross Hospital once a week for assessment. After the first week of light (two hours per day) I was so well that my daily dose was reduced to one hour per day for week two. I was still feeling fine by week three, so had a week without lights. By week four I still had not become depressed, so I tried another week without using light therapy. By week five, my mood had slumped considerably, so I was prescribed a daily dose of three hours light. This did the trick and kept me going till the end of the trial when

I bought my own light box and started using light therapy on a daily basis.

The six week trial was an invaluable experience for me for a number of reasons: it gave me a unique opportunity to have my depression, in all its different stages, closely monitored by expert and extremely caring doctors; it confirmed the fact that I have a genuine illness which I can justify to myself and everyone else; it brought an end to years of desperate seeking for an answer to my psychiatric problems and enabled me to start to tackle the other difficult areas in my life. Best of all, because of the unfailing support and reassurance I received during the trial and in the two years which followed, it ended my previous prejudices against doctors, and made me realize that they can be trusted rather than feared.

CHRYSTAL

I was one of the original 'guinea pigs' to be tested for SAD at the Maudsley Hospital under Dr Stuart Checkley during the winter 1985/86. Since then, I have had two wonderful winters: no pills, no overeating, therefore no weight gain. In the winter I have been as I am in the summer: active, energetic, sociable and confident. In fact you could say I have blossomed (as indeed have my geranium cuttings on the window near by light box). I am much better to live with altogether according to my long-suffering husband.

Although I started off with two hours treatment morning and evening, I now find I only need about one and a half hours morning and evening for the first two weeks of winter. Then as the season progresses I adjust the number of hours to suit my lifestyle and needs, gradually reducing or increasing it according to how I feel. Over the years I find I need to use it less. Some days if it is very sunny I do not use it at all. In fact, I consider myself to be a battery that needs a regular top up now and then.

PHILIP

I went into hospital for treatment just before Christmas. There were four of us, Anne, George, Margaret and myself. Before treatment our eyes were checked and photographed. Then we were assessed for thirty hours of light treatment, three hours in the morning and three hours at night, for five days.

The ward we were in was very friendly and we communicated regularly with the other patients there suffering from other kinds of depression. The staff were very helpful. George and I became friends and we used to have the therapy sessions together, the time passed quicker in company.

When the treatment was finished the psychiatrist said that he thought the lights would be beneficial to me. I was feeling so much better than when I went into hospital that I telephoned a distributor of lights immediately, collected them that evening and have used them ever since.

I had the best Christmas I could remember and I now know that the rest of the season passes very quickly with the lights. It is mid-winter, and I feel great. I haven't had to use any anti-depressants since I bought the light box.

9

Anti-depressant Medication

In the majority of cases light therapy is a highly effective treatment for SAD. However, for some people, the relief achieved is only partial. For this reason anti-depressant medication is sometimes prescribed which, when used in conjunction with light therapy, sometimes brings a more complete recovery. Specific drugs used to treat SAD can alleviate many of the common symptoms of depression and lack of energy and motivation. Some even control appetite cravings and thus help to prevent weight gain. Drug therapy can be useful to SAD patients who have difficulty incorporating light therapy into their daily schedule. Anti-depressant medication provides an alternative which is not as effective as light therapy, but is generally better than no treatment at all.

You may have already been treated with anti-depressants in the past. Until SAD became a recognised illness many sufferers were treated with anti-depressant medications or tranquillisers, many of which were unsuitable for the condition, and some of which made their symptoms worse. Because SAD is still a relatively new phenomenon (yet one which is rapidly becoming more known), it is essential if you want to try anti-depressants that you consult a doctor who is aware of SAD and of successful ways of treating it. The drugs prescribed for other types of depression are different from those most effective in treating SAD. If you are unsure of your doctor, ask to be referred to a SAD clinic, where you can consult a psychiatrist.

Many of us are automatically reluctant to take drugs,

especially those which induce mood changes. This may be the result of a bad experience in the past when you were misdiagnosed and wrongly prescribed; it may be a fear of the physical or mental changes which could occur as a result of taking the drugs; or it may be a resistance to admitting to depression and the need for treatment. While it is always necessary to be cautious about any medication, it is also wise to be open-minded. Learn about the drugs and their potential effects, and weigh up the advantages and disadvantages. Almost all drugs have side-effects, so it is generally a question of deciding which constitutes the most danger to your well being: the side-effects or the constant symptoms of SAD. Before making your decision consider some of these inaccurate preconceptions about anti-depressant medication.

'DRUGS ARE DANGEROUS'

There is no doubt that anti-depressant medication can be dangerous if taken at the wrong time or in the wrong dose. This is why it should be taken only under specialist supervision. When correctly monitored such medication rarely produces dangerous adverse reactions, although any unexpected or extreme side-effects should be reported to your doctor. Working together, you can then decide how to deal with them. It is important to remember that drugs can be dangerous, but so can SAD if it is left untreated.

'DRUGS MAKE ME FEEL DIFFERENT, I'M NOT MYSELF'

You may have been depressed for such a long time that it seems abnormal to feel well. If you are using the correct anti-depressant there is no reason why you should feel abnormally 'high', but every reason for you to feel less depressed and more enthusiastic about life. Consult your doctor if you experience unnatural symptoms – excessive elation or zombie-like sensations. You are probably taking the wrong drug.

'WHAT ABOUT THE SIDE-EFFECTS?'

It may take some time to find the right drug. It is a process of trial and error to discover the one which gives the most benefit and the least side-effects. Some anti-depressant medication produces unpleasant side-effects for the first few weeks, then the body gets used to it, and side effects subside. You may find it worthwhile to put up with this limited period of discomfort if the medication will eventually provide longterm relief. Discuss the problems with your doctor and weigh up the advantages and disadvantages.

'I MIGHT BECOME ADDICTED'

Anti-depressants should not be confused with tranquillizers and sleeping tablets. They are not addictive. Moreover, you will probably only be taking them during the winter months, not continuously. However, stick to the recommended dosage and do not suddenly stop taking them without consulting your doctor.

'I SHOULDN'T NEED ANTI-DEPRESSANTS'

This common reaction is tied to one of the predominant and most pervasive symptoms of SAD: guilt. Underlying this reaction is the thought that by taking anti-depressants you are admitting to a weakness, which should be avoided at all costs. Instead try to equate SAD with some other physical illness, diabetes, for example. Would you feel guilty about taking your daily dose of insulin? If you had high blood pressure would you be reluctant to take medication? These are genetic and biochemical diseases, in the same way as SAD. There is therefore no reason to let guilt prevent you from seeking out the best possible treatment.

Alternatively you may think that you should be able to deal with SAD on your own and that by taking anti-depressants you are letting yourself down. Whether this is so depends on the severity of your condition. In most cases light therapy and the programme advocated in this book will allow you to take control of your illness through self help. However, in some cases anti-depressant medication can provide a necessary trigger to allow self help to occur.

Here is an example of a SAD sufferer who found light therapy did not bring relief and instead used anti-depressant medication to combat SAD:

MARIANNE:

As far back as I can remember, I have suffered from swings of mood and lethargy during the winter months. I am 41 and have four lively children, an 85 year old mother-in-law living in, a large house to organize and, until last year, a business run from home. I was able to cope until about six years ago, when I had a fairly late miscarriage, followed by post-natal depression. Every winter since then I have had SAD symptoms which got progressively worse until last year when I sought medical help and was prescribed trimipramine (an anti-depressant drug), which lifted the depression rapidly.

I continued to feel fine until mid-autumn, but as winter encroached I had to admit that SAD was back again, despite my efforts to fight it. I bought a light box and persevered with treatment for three to four hours every evening, as I found it impossible to get up two hours earlier in the morning. However, I became more and more depressed and finally lost control. I found myself frequently in floods of tears for no apparent reason. My doctor put me back on trimipramine, but over the next fortnight I became worse. I'd go to sleep each night wishing I didn't have to wake up, but I had to keep going because of my family.

I spent hours drawing, which I found therapeutic, but I couldn't seem to organize the everyday chores, like washing and cooking. We were eating convenience foods and the family was washing the dishes and essential clothes. At this point my doctor changed the treatment from trimipramine to imipramine, and almost overnight I was a different person. I haven't looked back since. I feel well, optimistic about the future and have been accepted for a place on a two year, part-time art course. This starts in the autumn, so will give me something to look forward to during the darker months when I can always fall back on the non-addictive imipramine.

THE CHEMICAL CONNECTION

As we saw in Parts One and Two, many of the symptoms of SAD are related to an imbalance or disfunction of neurotransmitters (chemical nerve messengers) in the brain. The delicate balance of brain chemicals is regulated by the body's production of hormones. If this delicate balance is upset in some way symptoms such as depression, drowsiness or food cravings can occur. Different types of anti-depressant drugs act on neurotransmitters in different ways, to redress the imbalance. The type of medication you need will be decided in consultation with your doctor. The principal types used to treat SAD are described here in detail, and in table form for quick reference.

Tricyclic Anti-depressants

Desipramine = Norpramin/Pertofrane
Imipramine = Tofranil
These are the most commonly prescribed drugs for classical depression. Their action is thought to enhance neurotransmitter potency in the brain. Although in the past they have been used to treat SAD, they are not recommended now, owing

COMMON DRUGS USED TO TREAT SAD

DRUG (TRADE NAME)	DOSE	SIDE-EFFECTS WHICH SOMETIMES OCCUR
TRICYLICS Desipramine (Pertofrane)	100-150mg daily in divided doses	Trembling, dry mouth, blurred vision, constipation, passing water less often, dizziness.
Imiprimine (Tofranil)	100-150 mg daily	Similar to those caused by Desipramine.
MAOIs Phenelzine (Nardil)	15mg, 3 times daily. May be increased to 4 times daily after 2 weeks, then reduced to lowest possible maintenance dose	Dizziness, lower blood pressure, sometimes agitation, trembling, headache, constipation, blurred vision, passing water less often. Can cause rapid rise in blood pressure if combined with certain foods (see p.135)
Isocarboxazid (Marplan)	10-20mg daily	Similar to above. In rare cases may cause anaemia, swelling of ankles, kidney disease.
Tranylcypromine (Parnate)	10mg daily	Disturbed sleep, dizziness, muscle weakness, dry mouth, lower blood pressure. If rapid rise in blood pressure with severe headache, consult doctor immediately.
SEROTONIN ACTIVE ANTI-DEPRESSANTS Fluoxetine (Prozac)	20mg	Nausea, drowsiness, tremor, stomach upsets.
Fluvoxamine (Faverin)	100-300mg	Nausea, drowsiness, tremor.
LITHIUM CARBONATE (Camcolit, Phasal, Liskonium, Priadel)	250-2000mg Dose adjusted by regular blood tests	Stomach upsets with loose stools, increase in passing water, metallic taste. If visible shaking occurs, or increased thirst, vomiting or diarrhoea, consult doctor immediately.

to their sedative effect. They appear to bring drowsiness and increased appetite, thus enforcing rather than alleviating the typical SAD symptoms of fatigue and hunger. Common side-effects of tricyclic anti-depressants can be: dry mouth, blurred vision, constipation, difficulty passing water, weight gain.

Monoamine Oxidase Inhibitors (MAOIs)

Isocarboxazid = Marplan
Phenelzine = Nardil
Tranylcypromine = Parnate
Moclobemide = Manerix
MAOIs are thought to indirectly boost the production of brain neurotransmitters such as norepinephrine and sero-tonin, thus correcting any deficiency. They can be helpful for treating SAD because in most cases they energize rather than sedate. They can have mild side-effects. The most common ones are: dry mouth, insomnia, constipation, difficulty focusing, lightheadedness when standing suddenly, dizziness (take care when driving or operating machinery) and skin rashes. Certain foods and drinks cannot be consumed when taking MAOIs, as the combination can cause a sudden and dangerous rise in blood pressure. All foods which are partly spoiled should be avoided. Here is a basic list:

Cheese and yoghurt
Meat and yeast extracts, such as Marmite/Bovril/Oxo
Pickled fish
Marinated meats

Some cough and cold medications sold over the counter should also be avoided.

Your doctor will advise you which foods to avoid when prescribing your medication.

Selective Serotonin Reuptake Inhibitors (SSRIs)

Fluoxetine = Prozac
Sertraline = Lustral or Zoloft
Paroxetine = Seroxat or Paxil
These are relatively new medications and are presently the most popular choice for treating SAD if light therapy is not sufficient. They act by promoting the production of serotonin in the brain. We seem to produce less serotonin in winter than at any other time of the year (see Part Two). If it is deficient, depression and carbohydrate craving can result. By replacing serotonin deficiency, these drugs appear to have a double action of lifting mood and reducing carbohydrate consumption and weight gain. For the first two weeks serotonin active anti-depressants can produce side-effects, such as stomach upsets, tremors, nausea and headaches.

Lithium Carbonate

Camcolit, Phasal, Liskonium, Priadel
Lithium was originally used to prevent manic depression, that is highly variable swings of mood from depression to mania (see Chapters Six and Fourteen). Because some SAD sufferers experience extreme periods of highs and lows this medication can be helpful as an anti-depressant and a mood stabilizer. It can be used alone, or in combination with any of the drugs mentioned above. However, lithium intake has to be closely monitored by taking weekly blood samples. Too much can be toxic and result in convulsion, coma or even death. When properly monitored, side-effects are usually mild and include minor stomach upsets with loose stools, urine increase and a metallic taste in the mouth during the first few weeks. If side-effects persist or if you experience visible shaking, increased thirst, vomiting or diarrhoea consult your doctor immediately.

Other Drugs Your Doctor May Prescribe

Some doctors use minor tranquillizers or sedatives to treat nervousness and anxiety. Typical examples are Librium, Valium, Ativan, and Unisomnia. These are not advisable for SAD. They are addictive, and because they are sedatives they may worsen your symptoms.

Your doctor may however prescribe a major tranquillizer as a short-term measure while you are waiting for the effects of lithium carbonate to take place. Examples of major tranquillisers are Haloperidol or Chlorpromazine. Neither should be taken on a long-term basis.

Sleeping tablets are not advised for the treatment of SAD. When used regularly sleeping tablets lose their effect and the dosage has to be increased, which can lead to dependency. In limited cases they may help to establish a regular sleep pattern (see Chapter Eleven) but in most cases it is better to do without.

If you are already taking any of these types of medication do not stop them abruptly. Withdrawal must be done gradually, and under medical supervision.

THINGS YOU SHOULD KNOW ABOUT
ANTI-DEPRESSANTS

Many people find they have little relief from anti-depressants. One of the common reasons for this is that the dosage is too low. This may be the doctor's fault for under-prescribing, or your fault for not taking the recommended dose. If you insist on taking a dosage which is too low you are wasting your time. If you are taking the dose which is recommended, but still not getting any effect, return to your doctor to reassess the dosage. Never increase the dosage without medical supervision.

Remember, anti-depressant drugs take two to three weeks to take effect. If you are not getting immediate relief, do not give up before this time. However, if after a month of medication you still have no relief, you may be taking the wrong drug and should return to discuss the matter with your doctor.

Do not be alarmed if your doctor advises you to gradually increase the dose each day. With some drugs the best way to avoid side effects is to start out with a small dose, and gradually build up to the recommended amount over a week.

The most common side effects of anti-depressant medication for SAD are dry mouth, mild hand tremors, occasional lightheadedness and constipation. These usually occur in the first few weeks and then tend to diminish. Side effects which suggest you are taking excessive doses will be difficulty in urination, blurred vision, confusion, severe tremor, serious dizziness or increased perspiration. Consult your doctor if any of these occur.

The time at which you start or stop a medication will depend on you and your doctor. It is advisable to be drug free when first attempting light therapy so that you can assess the genuine effects. If you find that light therapy is not enough, or cannot be incorporated into your routine, anti-depressant medication may help you. In most cases of SAD anti-depressant medication is only a temporary measure. You will probably only need the treatment during the winter and can withdraw from it gradually in the spring or summer.

10

Talking and Relaxation Therapy

Your search for a cure for SAD or the winter blues may have brought you into contact with many of the physical and psychological therapies on offer today. Light therapy is indisputably the most effective and specialized treatment for SAD. However, a number of sufferers, once they are introduced to light therapy and find themselves on the road to recovery, become motivated to complement it with other techniques in order to achieve a total recovery of mind and body. This chapter brings together some of their suggestions.

TALKING THERAPY

You may by now have found a way to relieve the symptoms of SAD through light therapy or some of the other techniques outlined in this programme. While the recovery is welcome, it is not always enough to rebuild lives which have been dramatically scarred by recurrent winters of SAD. Immediate symptoms may be relieved, but underlying problems may remain: abandoned careers or broken marriages are not uncommon examples. The delight of finding a treatment for SAD can sometimes be marred by the pressure of knowing that you should therefore be able to make a success of life, despite your lack of self-confidence. You may feel disappointed that there are still factors in your life which continue to make you feel depressed and miserable. You may start to recognize patterns of behaviour which seem out of your control. Or perhaps you suddenly see opportunities which you still can't quite realize.

Talking to a professional who is qualified to analyse problems and give guidance has helped many SAD sufferers adapt to the changes brought by light therapy. In some cases this means rebuilding lives and starting again. Talking therapy can be divided up into three professional categories:

- COUNSELLING: the opportunity to discuss current problems with a therapist who is trained to listen and give advice.
- PSYCHOTHERAPY: the opportunity to discuss thoughts, emotions and problems with a therapist who will employ different techniques to help you to understand your behaviour and thoughts. For example, why you feel unhappy or why you are unable to achieve what you want in life. The aim of this is to search for and overcome the underlying obstacles to self fulfilment.
- PSYCHOANALYSIS: a longterm and specialized type of psychotherapy based along the beliefs of psychoanalytic theorists such as Freud, Jung and Klein.

Talking therapy offers the opportunity to talk frankly and fearlessly to a trained and sympathetic ear; someone who can help analyse emotions, behaviour and situations and focus you in the right direction to solve problems. In so doing it helps unravel the cause of difficulties and simplify them. It helps you to discover aspects of your character or life, which may be holding you back from doing what you want to do. By becoming aware of these aspects through self-observation you will slowly be able to make changes and adapt to a new way of thinking and seeing yourself and the world.

At this point you may be wondering what it would be like to talk to a total stranger about your most personal feelings. Why not confide in a friend? Friends can certainly provide the opportunity to discuss problems, they can also provide useful suggestions. But they cannot be expected to sort out longterm difficulties or help you look back at past experiences. Although they may be sympathetic, they cannot provide the patience offered by a professional talking therapist. Pouring out your problems to friends on a regular basis could be detrimental to your relationship.

Furthermore, what we say is not always what we mean; it takes a trained professional to interpret emotions which can show themselves in different ways. Friends can provide relief and support, but they are often too close to you to make an objective, truthful analysis of your situation in order to allow for change. Therapists, on the other hand, maintain an emotional distance. They are paid to be at your disposal during the time of your appointment, and there is no question that you have to fulfil the mutual obligations of a friendship. Everything you say to a therapist will be kept in total confidence; the therapist has no interest in casting judgements. However, he/she will recognize and challenge you when you are not true to yourself.

Who to Talk to?

Attitudes to counselling and psychotherapy have drastically changed over the last ten years. Originally looked down on as an over-indulgent and unnecessary means of alleviating emotional disturbances, these therapies are now accepted as a fashionable route to self-discovery and fulfilment. The confusing number of different types and techniques make finding a suitable therapist a daunting procedure.

In some countries, such as Britain, talking therapy is sometimes offered by the health service. In others you can claim the expense on insurance. If you seek therapy through the health service you will probably have to go through your doctor. He/she may refer you to a;

- PSYCHIATRIST: This is a medical doctor who specializes in psychiatric illness. In Britain every area has its own psychiatrist who works in the local hospital and is responsible for the psychological care of his/her area. Many psychiatrists are trained to do psychoanalysis, but rarely have time to do it. They are more likely to refer you to a:
- CLINICAL PSYCHOLOGIST: this is not a doctor, but a person who has a degree in psychology and several years of clinical training. Some have also carried out research and have PhDs, so hold the title 'Doctor'. Psychologists may offer short-term counselling, or longer-term psychotherapy.

Alternatively you may be referred to a:

- COUNSELLOR: this is a person trained to help you deal with immediate problems and anxieties, such as financial difficulties or marital problems.

If you decide to consult a private therapist, you will have more choice about who you see and will not have to wait for treatment. Your doctor or psychiatrist may be able to recommend a private counsellor or psychotherapist. Whether the person you seek is a private therapist, or working as part of a national health service, it is essential that they are aware of SAD. Some are not and it is pointless to pursue therapy with someone who is not conscious of your condition and needs.

Looking for a Private Therapist

Your choice of therapist will depend somewhat on your location and the time you are prepared to spend looking. It is worth remembering that the success of the therapy will depend both on the competence of the therapist and whether he/she is compatible with you. Many people wait until they are at crisis point and call the first number listed in the telephone directory. While the outcome of this approach may in some cases be entirely satisfactory, your frantic condition could mar your judgement of a therapist's competence or compatibility.

One of the best ways to find a therapist is to seek out recommendations. Talk to organisations, support groups, health professionals, friends who have been in therapy. Get a feel for what the therapist they recommend is like. Ask basic questions about their sex and age, where they practice, what they charge and how the sessions are conducted.

Once you have a few names and telephone numbers there is no reason why you cannot call directly and find out more. Most good therapists are busy people and you are likely to be confronted by an answering machine. Do not be put off, you can leave a message requesting them to ring you back. Alternatively, you may catch the therapist at a busy moment, and have to arrange a time to speak which is more convenient. Make sure you do speak to the therapist, not to an intermediary person; the aim of your phone call is not only to obtain factual information, but also to gain a first impression of the person you will be dealing with. The therapist will probably not want to discuss your case in detail on the phone, and will instead wish to arrange an appointment. However, the telephone call is your opportunity to ask certain brief questions and find out more about the therapist.

Here are some preliminary questions you should ask:

- Does the therapist have time to see you on a regular basis in hours which are convenient to you?
- What does the therapist charge?
- What kind of training has the therapist had: what qualifications does he/she hold and how long has he/she been practising?
- Where does the therapist practice?

You are perfectly at liberty to ask brief questions. If the telephone interview goes well, you may agree to an initial appointment. On the other hand, you may wish first to investigate some other recommendations. A professional therapist will not be offended by your caution in coming to a decision.

The First Visit

Your first visit to a therapist will allow you to get to know him/her more, to explain why you want therapy and to assess his/her reaction to your needs. It should also give the therapist the opportunity to decide if he/she can be of help.

How comfortable you feel with the therapist and the surroundings will help in your decision making. It is always difficult to talk to a stranger about emotional or personal matters. It is likely that the therapist will not push or pry for information, but let you reveal what you want and no more. The extent to which the therapist puts you at ease during this process will determine how compatible you are.

Consider these points during the first session:

- Do you gradually loosen up during the session, or do you get more tense?
- Does the therapist give you the opportunity to speak, or constantly interrupt?
- Does the therapist look interested in what you say?
- Does the therapist accept your right to ask questions?
- Do the answers he/she gives seem satisfactory and meaningful?
- Does the therapist look and act like a person you would respect?
- Do you like the therapist?

Your instinctive reaction is probably the best one to follow at this stage. You will probably know by the end of the session if you think it will be possible and profitable to continue therapy with this person and it is up to you to ask for another appointment. If you are unsure, however, do not be afraid to delay your decision and telephone at a later date.

What Happens in Talking Therapy?

What happens during your sessions depends on the type of talking therapy. If you are seeing a counsellor, you will probably start by explaining current difficulties and problems in your life. Together you will discuss them and work out practical solutions. If you are seeing a psychologist, psychotherapist or psychoanalyst, you will be encouraged to talk more about your feelings: your thoughts, reactions, fears, expectations, disappointments, and fantasies. Through talking you will provide the material for self-exploration, you will initiate ideas, arouse feelings and memories and relieve anxieties.

Talking is not the only means of communication in therapy. Although most of us have the capacity to relate everyday events, when it comes to expressing emotions or sensations we may not have the words or the ability to do so. In such cases the therapist may suggest other media of expression: drawing, imaging, role playing, body movement, for example. Often these forms of expression, which come from the subconscious, are more truthful than the spoken word.

The therapist's job is to help direct you towards self awareness and self change. He/she is trained to make suggestions which point you in the right direction for problem solving. He/she will make you aware of your cognitive errors, your associations and your inconsistencies. He/she may ask questions which you would not have considered asking yourself. All this will help you to become aware of your reactions and feelings and see them in a different light, with the aim of becoming more comfortable with yourself and your life.

STRESS MANAGEMENT

The wintertime change in mood and energy level associated with SAD can be extremely stressful. Life becomes a burden, and you may not be able to cope with the pressure and anxiety it brings. SAD sufferers are often high achievers, and consequently when they are unable to maintain their high standards during the winter they become anxious and frustrated. A vicious circle develops, in which fatigue and depression make you unable to cope with the normal demands of life. The result is stress. Stress is not just a state of mind, but a physical reaction which gobbles up energy and in turn leads to further exhaustion. Many SAD sufferers have found that by discarding unnecessary causes of stress, they can increase their energy. Here are some of their suggestions:

Organizing Stress

If you suffer from SAD you know that your energy level will be higher in summer than in winter. You must therefore attempt as far as possible to eliminate obvious stressful events from your life in the winter and transfer them to the summer. This may not always be possible as stress often strikes when we are least expecting it, but there are certain predictable situations which you can avoid.

- Try to reserve potentially stressful undertakings for the summer months when you have the most energy. For example, moving house or location, looking for or starting a new job, travelling, embarking on a new project, dealing with a problem, confronting a relationship.
- Plan ahead. Try to anticipate the burdens you will be faced with in the winter, and deal with some of them in the summer months. For example, if you are in the northern hemisphere you could try to prepare for Christmas early. Do your shopping and card writing in the summer. If you have a large freezer you could even prepare meals ahead, cooking in the summer for the autumn and winter. Clothes shopping is another stressful occupation which can be

done in spring or summer rather than winter. Some winter sales continue into the spring. When your energy starts to return look out for winter bargains. Similarly, the new winter season clothing often appears in the shops at the end of summer. You do not have to shop in winter.

The next step is to locate and discard any other unnecessary sources of stress which lower your energy. This is a rule which should apply the whole year round, but is particularly important in winter.

It is important, when seeking to eliminate anxiety, to distinguish between stress which provides a challenge and stress which you could do without. When you are suffering from SAD this distinction may be difficult as everything will probably seem too much to cope with. However, once light therapy has restored some of your energy, look at the sources of continued stress in your life. Think carefully about whether a particular stress is caused by a challenge you would really like to meet, or whether it is something which is burdening your life. Areas in which it is useful to look for sources of stress include work, financial demands, responsibility to family and friends, social commitments.

For example, Pauline always used to arrange the office Christmas meal. She felt it her duty to continue with this task, but on careful consideration realised it was causing her a great deal of stress in winter, with little reward or enjoyment. She felt guilty refusing to do it, but finally was persuaded to pass the responsibility to someone else. Once this decision had been made she felt extremely relieved. No-one resented her sharing the responsibility.

Small stresses like this one can be eliminated fairly swiftly once you manage to identify them. However, when considering major changes, take time to reflect. Wait until several winters have passed before you do anything drastic like changing job or location, or abandoning a friend or partner.

Sometimes it is better to learn to live with stress than to make changes which will make life more difficult. You can learn techniques which will teach you to expend less energy on stressful situations and to turn stress to your advantage.

First it is important to recognize the signs of stress. Physical signs are increased perspiration, racing heart and feeling jittery. Sometimes your stomach may tighten or you get diarrhoea, you may develop neck or back pains, or headaches. Mental signs include an inability to concentrate, feelings of panic and despair, indecision and fear of failure.

Ways of Coping with Stress

- DIVERSION: Try to distract yourself when you become obsessed with a stressful thought. One of the best ways of doing this is to talk to others about something other than what is causing you stress. If this doesn't work try to ask yourself the question 'What is the worst thing that can happen?' Recognizing the consequences of a concern and bringing it into perspective can help relieve tension.
- EXERCISE: Medical research has proved that vigorous exercise taken regularly alters mood and reduces tension. One study found that as little as fifteen minutes walking each day is more efficient in relieving stress than a course of tranquillisers. In addition, if you are physically fit your body is better able to cope with the pressure of stress.
- LEARN TO DEAL WITH HASSLES: Try to identify the small things in your life which make you uptight, such as being late, or waiting for others who are late, travelling in the rush hour, waiting in queues, someone not putting the cap on the toothpaste. Small as they may seem, these minor aggravations all add to our stress levels. Try to keep a record of the things which make you feel stressful or anxious over a week, and look at how you deal with them. Being aware of them may be enough to avoid some of them

all together. You may be able to resolve those which involve other people by gently explaining the stressful effect they are having on you. Such an explanation is far more effective than a submissive silence or an angry outburst.

- FIND OUT WHAT HELPS YOU UNWIND: This should be pleasurable as well as relaxing. It may be shutting yourself in the bathroom for a candlelit bath, it may be watching a film or reading a magazine or novel, it may be having a haircut or a facial, it may be a walk in the country. It is important to know what helps you unwind and to use them when you feel stress mounting.

BODY THERAPY

Mental stress can lead to physical discomfort. One of the principal causes of neck pain and backache is tension. When we are under stress we hold our bodies in stiff, unnatural stances and thus put joints and muscles under strain. Tension leads to restricted blood supply to the muscles, and hence to reduced oxygen supply, stiffening and fatigue. Many people suffering from stress find that body therapies, such as massage, aromatherapy or shiatsu give relief from such strain. All these therapies use types of massage to increase blood circulation in the body, soften tightened muscles, and loosen stiff joints. Once the body is able to relax physically, mental relaxation follows naturally. Massage often has an immediate sedative effect, but later brings increased energy.

RELAXATION TECHNIQUES

You can learn techniques which induce mental and physical relaxation. When practised regularly, these provide the ability to move into a temporary state of deep stillness or meditation in which outside thoughts and concerns are replaced by an awareness of a quiet centre within. Many studies carried out on people who have been taught relaxation techniques show that mental and physical changes take place in the body within about twenty minutes of practice. Tests have shown that relaxation techniques calm the body, reduce oxygen demand, slow the heartbeat and change brainwave patterns. Meditation, yoga, autogenic training, and biofeedback are just some of the possible tools which help achieve relaxation.

11

Fighting Depression

As we saw in Part Two, depression is one of the most pervasive of SAD symptoms. Its onset is often unnoticed; it begins with irritability and turns to feelings of guilt, inadequacy and total despondency. While light therapy is helpful in alleviating such feelings, it is important to be aware of the onset of depression, and check it before it gets a grip. This chapter describes self-help techniques which you can use to complement light therapy. We propose five exercises which will allow you to:

- identify and get to know your symptoms
- attack negative thinking
- regain confidence
- reduce the demands of others and your own self-expectations
- take positive steps to bring yourself out of depression

At first these exercises may take a little time. They require you to examine your ways of thinking and to get to know yourself. However, once you have done them several times you will find yourself automatically employing them at moments when you feel yourself slipping into depression. The exercises will arm you with tools to control depression before it controls you.

IDENTIFY YOUR SYMPTOMS

First it is important to recognize how depression affects you. Below are some symptoms which may correspond to your feelings during the winter. Write down any which seem familiar to you. By writing down how you feel, you will recognize how real the symptoms are and this will encourage you to take steps to change them.

Despair

- MILD: You experience feelings of sadness, which fluctuate with more cheerful feelings initiated by outside stimuli such as a compliment, a joke, or a favourable event.
- SEVERE: You constantly feel sad and find no relief in external events, ideas or people. This is often accompanied by a sense of hopelessness and misery, or even a feeling that the pain of sadness is too much to bear.

Loss of Zest for Life

- MILD: Simple satisfactions in life are lost. The displeasure may arise originally from responsibilities or obligations, although you can still find relief in increased rest and entertainment.
- SEVERE: You lose interest in all pleasures, even those afforded by achievement, a favourite entertainment, rest or meetings with friends. Life becomes totally devoid of happiness or satisfaction and no longer seems worth living.

Self-negativity and Loss of Self-esteem

- MILD: You tend to dislike how you look and what you are, and assume everyone else does: 'no one likes me, they're just tolerating me' are common feelings. You sense disappointment and guilt about letting people down, or not trying hard enough at some task. Your self-confidence dwindles.

- SEVERE: The dislike for yourself turns to hatred and you become guilt-ridden, blaming yourself for issues outside your control. This may be expressed in tentatively suicidal phrases such as 'I don't deserve to live, I hate myself'.

Loss of Emotional Attachment

- MILD: You lose interest in friends, family and loved ones. Your desire for sexual contact decreases and relationships may become less intense or loving.
- SEVERE: The lack of intensity turns to indifference or even hatred for those upon whom you are dependent.

Crying Spells

- MILD: Weeping tends to occur in situations which normally would not initiate tears, such as during a minor dispute or mishap. The incidence increases so you sometimes end up crying dozens of times a day.
- SEVERE: You want to cry but cannot.

Loss of Motivation

- MILD: You lose interest in social activities, hobbies and work. You feel you are operating mechanically without incentive, having to force yourself all the time. Concentration is difficult, and you rarely finish projects you have started.
- SEVERE: Even activities such as preparing meals and attending to personal hygiene are neglected, as you become more and more inactive, preferring to stay in bed alone.

You may by now have formulated a list of the symptoms which sum up your feelings in winter. Add to the list any other symptoms of depression you experience which were not mentioned in the list above.

Writing down your symptoms will assist in two things: it will help you to accept that you suffer from depression, and it will make you more familiar with your symptoms. Being more aware of how depression affects you, the symptoms will not catch you unawares next time they strike.

Now that you have accepted your symptoms, you can look at what triggers and sustains your depression and learn how to control it.

RECOGNIZE YOUR COGNITIVE ERRORS

In Chapter Six you read about the distortions in thinking or cognitive errors which are characteristic of depression. These negative and often irrational thoughts become obsessive when we are depressed and they help to nurture feelings of low self-esteem and guilt.

SAD sufferers often make the same cognitive errors consistently, so they can easily be recognized. Here is a list of some of the thinking errors which are most commonly made. Do you recognize any? If so, write them down.

- ALL OR NOTHING THINKING: You see things in black and white categories. For example if your performance falls short of perfect, you see yourself as a total failure.

- OVERGENERALIZATION: You see a single negative event as an inevitable pattern of defeat. For example if your girlfriend/boyfriend leaves, you imagine that all future relationships will end in disaster.

- MENTAL FILTER: You pick out a single negative detail and dwell on it exclusively, thus perceiving the whole situation as negative. For example, if you make one mistake at an interview you blow it out of proportion and assume you have ruined your chances, despite having other attributes which may qualify you for the job.

- DISQUALIFYING THE POSITIVE: You ignore positive experiences and transform them into negative ones. For example, if someone pays you a compliment, you react suspiciously, thinking or claiming it was not made in sincerity. Alternatively, you make excuses insisting you are not qualified to receive the praise, thus reinforcing your lack of self-esteem.

- JUMPING TO CONCLUSIONS: You make a negative interpretation even though there are no definite facts that convincingly support your conclusion. For example, you may be talking to a group of people and one of them yawns, so you immediately jump to the conclusion that everyone thinks you are boring. You do not consider that the yawning individual may have had a late night. You telephone a friend, leave a message and he does not ring you back; you automatically assume it is because he does not want to see or speak to you, you don't consider he might not have received the message.

- MAGNIFICATION (CATASTROPHIZING) OR MINIMIZATION: You exaggerate the importance of things (such as a mistake you made, or someone else's achievement), or you inappropriately shrink things (such as your own desirable qualities or another person's imperfections) until they appear tiny.

- EMOTIONAL REASONING: You assume that your negative emotions reflect the way things really are. For example, you feel guilty, therefore you assume you must have done something bad, or you feel inadequate, therefore you believe you are incapable. This kind of cognitive error leads to procrastination and the attitude 'I'm no good, therefore there is no point in doing anything'.

- 'SHOULD' STATEMENTS: You punish yourself by saying 'I should do this' or 'I must do that'. The result is that you end up feeling apathetic, unmotivated and guilty. When you direct 'should' statements towards others you feel anger, frustration and resentment.

- LABELLING AND MISLABELLING: This is an extreme form of overgeneralization. Instead of accepting your error, you attach a negative label to yourself: 'I'm a failure.' When someone else's behaviour rubs you the wrong way, you attach a negative label to him/her. Mislabelling sometimes involves describing an event with language that is inaccurate and often emotionally loaded.

- PERSONALIZATION: You see yourself as the cause of some negative external event that you were not in fact primarily responsible for. For example, if someone has an accident after leaving your house, you may blame yourself, rather than other factors which were probably involved.

(Table adapted from Burns, D., Feeling Good The New Mood Therapy, *William Morrow, New York 1980)*

ATTACK NEGATIVE THOUGHTS

Most of us make at least a few of these cognitive errors when we are feeling low. Often we are so wrapped up in our depression that we are unaware of making them. The following exercise will help you to determine which errors occur in your own thinking. Once you have identified the errors which occur time after time, you can take steps towards correcting them and find alternative ways of viewing the world.

The first step in the exercise is to think back over an event that you associate with feeling depressed. Write a short paragraph, giving a factual description of the event. For example, imagine that your car ran out of petrol: describe how it happened, where you were, etc. Now write another paragraph describing how the event made you feel. Did you feel angry, hopeless, incapable, victimized etc.

Now take a few moments to close your eyes and visualize the event. Attempt to sense the negative feelings you felt at that moment. Follow this up by writing down exactly how you feel, the thoughts which automatically come to mind. Don't even stop to think about it, just let the thoughts flow.

The next step in this exercise is to assess your thinking. Read through the paragraph of automatic thoughts highlighting those which seem illogical. For example, a logical thought would be annoyance with yourself for knowing that the tank was empty and not bothering to fill it up. If, on the other hand, the incident made you feel like a total failure, for whom nothing ever goes right, you are making a cognitive error of overgeneralization. Another cognitive error would be for you to view running out of petrol as a total disaster which will ruin your whole day, making it worthless to try anything else or even to exist. Thus is would be an error of magnification. Try to relate each of the illogical thoughts with one of the cognitive distortions listed above.

The next step is to find an alternative response to that of the cognitive distortion you have uncovered. Once you are aware of the thinking error you have made, rationalizing the problem will become easier. Write down a logical response as an alternative to each of the cognitive distortions you made. While doing this try to step aside and view the problem as an outsider. Rationalize the problem, not as if it were yours, but as if you were advising a friend on how to approach it. Once you have written it down, compare it to the original response you had to the event, and assess which is the most credible.

At first this procedure may seem long-winded and tedious, but after carrying it out a few times you may become aware of the patterns which your thoughts take when you are depressed. We all make cognitive errors, but the sooner we are aware of making them, the easier it is to break the habit and look at the world from a different perspective.

MODIFY GOALS

Becoming aware of cognitive errors and correcting them is the first step in conquering depression. It will also help lift self-confidence. However, such steps will be futile if you do not have the energy to maintain that confidence. Becoming tired and letting yourself down by attempting to achieve too much will immediately bring your mood crashing down again. Instead, you must accept that winter puts certain limitations on what you can do and how much you can achieve, and accept that your energy levels are not the same as they are in the spring and summer.

This means modifying goals and expectations. Right now you may be taking on too much and feeling guilty, frustrated and useless when you don't manage to complete the tasks you set yourself. Instead you need to limit your expectations so that you can sustain a sense of achievement during the winter as well as during the summer. The following paragraphs suggest a number of practical strategies which will help you to reduce your goals and expectations and, in turn, boost your self-esteem and lift depression.

First establish what your aims are this winter in terms of:

- daily accomplishments and quality of things you do (professionally and domestically)
- social commitments
- organizational responsibilities: meetings and entertaining, for example
- a personal relationship

Now tackle these expectations day by day. Draw up a list of all the things you have to do today. Put the entire list into rank order, starting with the item which will have the worst consequences if you don't accomplish it today. Give every item a rank number. Beginning with number one tackle the list.

Focus your attention only on that item until you have done as much as you can on it. Only then consider doing the next item on the list. It is advisable not to tackle more than three or four items a day.

Make another list of pleasurable activities which you want to do. When you get stuck on the items you have to do, switch to the list of items you want to do. Try to do at least three on this list per day.

Most SAD sufferers have high expectations of what they will get through in a day. You will probably feel less frustrated if you accept that your list is impossible to get through and content yourself with only three of the most important tasks. Tomorrow update your list and ranking system and start again at the top. You may not complete the list, in fact there are some things you will probably never get done, but at least you will achieve the most important tasks and feel in control of your day.

LEARN TO SAY 'NO'

Because of the guilt that envelopes all those suffering depression, refusing a request or demand is even more difficult when you are depressed than when not, even though you may feel less like complying. The way to look at it is this: the more things you do for others the less you do for yourself; the less you achieve for yourself, the more your self-confidence plummets and the worse you feel. As part of your winter programme you have to make a mental commitment to reduce the number of things you do for others. But how?

The first step is to write down several requests which you would like to refuse. For example, your mother-in-law wants to come and stay for a week, or your friend wants you to take a look at his broken exhaust pipe. Next to each request write down a sentence which refuses the request. Take care to formulate a response which is firm, but not apologetic or aggressive. Keep in mind the fact that you are reducing your own workload and expectations in order to preserve precious energy and remember, your time is your own to do what you please.

Next, practice saying the refusal, out loud if you can. Accustom yourself to hearing the sound of your own voice making it. By being prepared for what you are going to say, and confident that it sounds assertive but not hostile, you will find making refusals a lot easier. In addition, people will not regard you as being selfish with your time, but will respect your ability to choose what is best for you.

LEARN TO DELEGATE

In the same way as you learn how to refuse requests, so you can learn to delegate tasks which could conceivably be done by others. Make a list of jobs which could be delegated and to whom. Next to each one write down your request. Depending on the context, you may wish to explain that you suffer from SAD and need help in the winter. Prepare and practice how and what you are going to say.

Recognize that you are not capable of doing all that you can in the summer. You have already reduced your expectations and goals, but if you are still under pressure try to find help. For many women, getting help with the housework or children can provide an immense relief at this time of the year. If you cannot afford to pay for help, perhaps you can negotiate a deal with family or friends whereby you can reciprocate in the spring or summer months. If you cannot get help, then you will have to reduce your expectations further. Perhaps the housework will not get done so often during the winter months, perhaps you will have to make do more often with frozen and convenience foods. These are measures you must take to relieve yourself of the stress which undoubtedly adds to your depression. Once you have more time for yourself, then you will be able to concentrate on attacking negative thoughts and work towards positive action. Doing this will, in turn, lift your mood and allow you to take on more and more as you feel better.

POSITIVE ACTIONS

We have already looked at how to attack negative thinking. Next is positive action. The aim of the following exercise is to encourage you to engage in actions which you would do if you were in a more positive mood, such as socializing, or exercizing. The reason for doing this is that if you engage in activities which are incompatible with your mood, then your mood will be forced to correct itself in order to keep up with the activity in hand. Therefore, pursuing activities which are characteristic of positive moods will help lift your depression.

One of the most effective ways of carrying out this exercise is to engage in physical activity. A common symptom of depression is the desire to stay in bed or at home and refuse to venture out. Engaging in physical activity will force these feelings to give way to more pleasant and dynamic thoughts. If you have difficulty motivating yourself to leave the bed or house, remember that, if you feel terrible indoors or in bed, it cannot be any worse outside! It is crucial that you get out during the day and, if possible, take part in physical activity. In this way you can also benefit from an added dose of light. Because of the importance of getting outside and exercising, this subject is dealt with separately in Chapter Fifteen.

One of the last things we feel like doing when depressed is meeting and talking to other people, who always seem to be on top of the world. Consequently there is a tendency to withdraw from all contact and focus even more on the problems we face. One of the ways to alter this isolation is to attempt gradually to see more people. Start with a close friend, preferably someone who understands your feelings. The meeting does not have to be a long one, perhaps a lunch or coffee break. Try to take an interest in what he/she is saying by asking questions. Do not see the meeting as an opportunity to talk about your own mood. Make a mental note to do this at least once a week. You may find that over time your depression is lifted by mixing with others in better spirits and your desire to socialize becomes more frequent.

Because your energy is low when you are depressed, it will seem you have little time or inclination to engage in pleasurable activities. Indeed if you are severely depressed nothing will seem enjoyable. However, if you can manage to relieve yourself of some of your commitments during the winter, perhaps you should use this time to take part in activities which will allow relaxation and pleasure. Even if this idea does not rouse much enthusiasm, write down at least ten things which you would find pleasurable. Try to vary the list with things which take as little as ten minutes, such as browsing through your favourite magazine, and others which may require more time and planning, such as a weekend break or a holiday. At the beginning of each day, when you compile your list of things to be done, be sure to include as a high priority at least one of the pleasurable activities. Even if you do not feel like doing it, make time for it and carry it through.

The more you recognize how SAD affects your mood the more you will be able to do something about it. There is no doubt that these exercises require motivation. It is not sufficient to do them once, they must be done over and over again until you are able to immediately recognize how SAD affects your thinking and your perception of the world. The more you carry out these exercises the more effortless they will become, until eventually you are in the position to combat depression every time it rears its ugly head.

12

Winter Eating

SAD sufferers experience a marked change in eating habits during the winter months. Appetite increases and food preferences change. Winter brings a desire for more frequent meals and cravings for carbohydrates in the form of sugary or starchy foods. Both symptoms lead to an inevitable and often unwanted increase in weight. Yet, as we saw in Chapter Six, SAD sufferers rarely eat for pleasure or greed, but rather to gain relief from their other symptoms of tension, anxiety or fatigue. By eating carbohydrates they become calm and energized.

There is no doubt that what we eat and drink influences our mood and energy level. Therefore, by discovering more about which nutrients initiate which reactions, perhaps we could have greater control over how we feel. The rest of this chapter suggests ways of determining how food affects you and when. The suggestions and exercises will help you to establish which foods tend to make you depressed and drowsy and which maintain alertness and concentration. We are not proposing a crash diet or a programme of eating designed to lose weight, but rather a process of self discovery which will allow you to use food to control your energy and mood. This, in turn, will give you the opportunity to establish an individual eating programme suited to your winter condition.

HOW DO YOU REACT TO FOOD?

The first step in this programme is to allow yourself the freedom to find out how food affects your mood. As winter approaches you probably know that your eating habits will change and that you will gain weight. Your first reaction is probably to ensure the cupboards are free from sugary temptations and the fridge stocked with low calorie alternatives. Such measures could be denying your body the very nutrients it needs, and may make your symptoms worse. So, instead of depriving yourself, you must learn to allow your body what it wants in a disciplined way. The following exercise will help establish which foods you really need in the winter, in what quantity, and at what time of day.

You are now going to test your reaction to two principal nutrients: protein and carbohydrate. As we saw in Chapter Six, these are the two types of food which stimulate the production of serotonin, norepinephrine and dopamine, brain chemicals which affect how we feel: our levels of activity and our mood.

To carry out this test stock up the fridge with a selection of your favourite foods. Make sure you have enough protein to make at least seven pure protein meals: these can be meat, cheese, fish or egg based or, for vegetarians, pulses or tofu. Buy enough carbohydrates for at least seven carbohydrate meals. These could be pasta, potato, bread or rice based, served with cooked or raw vegetables, or topped with vegetable sauces. Finally, if you know you have a tendency to eat in between meals, buy a selection of your favourite individual snacks, either sweet or savoury, to last you the week.

Your next purchase is a large notepad or desk diary. This is to record what you eat and when, and to note how the food affects you during this experimental week. The aim is to record how you feel before eating, to list exactly what you eat, and finally to record how you feel one hour after eating.

Use these headings as guidelines to assess your moods before and after eating.

tired	alert	calm
lethargic	refreshed	relaxed
anxious	energetic	able to
depressed	enthusiastic	concentrate
tearful		
agitated		

During the experimental week you will alternate between pure protein and pure carbohydrate meals, noting the effects of each. Try to arrange your week according to the following plan:

- DAY 1: carbohydrate breakfast
  protein lunch
  carbohydrate dinner
- DAY 2: protein breakfast
  carbohydrate lunch
  protein dinner

On day three begin again at day one, and repeat the cycle until the end of the week.

The quantities of food you eat do not matter too much. What is important is to ensure that you do not mix protein and carbohydrate in one meal. Remember proteins are generally animal products, they are also found in pulses, such as beans or lentils; carbohydrates are starches and sugars. It is advisable to avoid alcohol for this week as this may influence your mood, although coffee and tea intake can remain the same as usual.

Overleaf are some guidelines for the foods you could choose from:

CARBOHYDRATE BREAKFASTS:
   coffee or tea with or without sugar
   toast with butter or low fat spread, jam, honey or marmalade
   oatmeal with skimmed milk and honey

PROTEIN BREAKFASTS:
   coffee or tea without sugar
   eggs
   kipper and tomato
   low fat yoghurt
   cottage cheese

CARBOHYDRATE LUNCH/DINNER
   baked potato with butter/sour cream and salad
   pasta with tomato or herb sauce
   rice with vegetables
   salad sandwich
   followed by
   cake, biscuit, dessert (try to avoid cream)
   drink of choice

PROTEIN LUNCH/DINNER
   baked, grilled or poached fish (for a cold lunch, tuna or sardines)
   grilled meat with fat removed
   eggs
   low fat cheese
   pulses
   tofu
   green cooked vegetables or salad
   followed by
   low fat yoghurt
   1 piece of fresh fruit
   sugar-free drink

You are free to take small protein or carbohydrate snacks in between meals. However, try not to snack until at least two hours after the main meals of the day, and ensure you note down what you eat, the time and its effects on your mood thirty minutes to an hour later.

ESTABLISH YOUR NUTRITIONAL NEEDS

Your notes will give you the information you need to establish how you react to food. At the end of the week look back at your reactions to the different meals. Did you notice any change in mood, before and after eating? What was the change? Compare the reactions you had after eating a protein lunch with those experienced after eating a carbohydrate lunch. How did you feel after protein or carbohydrate snacks?

In research trials it has been noted that some people find protein meals give them energy, whereas carbohydrates make them drowsy. Others, however, find that carbohydrates stimulate them, making them feel less drowsy and more able to concentrate, SAD sufferers often fall into the latter category, which explains their craving for sweet and starchy foods when they are tired or depressed. From your experimental notes you may notice a pattern of how the different nutrients affect you. The results of this experiment will determine the basis for your future eating plan. If protein is the nutrient which energizes and invigorates you, while carbohydrates bring fatigue and dullness, then your morning and midday meals should be predominantly protein-based, and carbohydrates should be left for times when you wish to relax or sleep. If, however, you find carbohydrate meals or snacks bring renewed energy when you are flagging and allow you to concentrate better, then they should be generously incorporated into your eating schedule throughout the day.

Your notes will also inform you of the time you most need these nutrients. For example, if your diary shows that each day around 4 or 5 pm you reach for the chocolate bars, this could be the time when you most need carbohydrate. This need should not be ignored but, instead, incorporated into your daily eating plan.

Once you have established how food affects your mood you can formulate an eating programme which will give you protein or carbohydrate when you most need it. Don't forget that your energy will be affected by the amount of food you eat and when you eat it as well as the type of nutrient. Heavy foods, such as rich proteins and fats require much energy to digest and leave us feeling exhausted. Eating light meals which incorporate vegetables rather than fats may be less taxing. Below are some basic guidelines which you can adapt according to your tastes and needs.

Breakfast

It is important to eat something before midday, otherwise you will be tempted to overeat at lunchtime, and this could cause an unwanted afternoon slump in energy.

Suggested foods: fresh fruit or juice, yoghurt, cereal or oatmeal with low fat milk, eggs, cheese, wholemeal bread, tea or coffee.

Lunch

By lunchtime your energy may be on the wane, so you need food which will keep the brain active. What you eat will depend on how you react to protein and carbohydrate:

- If you find protein energizing, keep carbohydrates to a minimum and concentrate on light proteins like low fat meats, cheeses and fish, pulses or soya and plenty of vegetables. Have fruit or low fat yoghurt for dessert.

- If you find carbohydrates energizing, choose starchy rather than sugar foods. For example, potatoes, wholemeal bread, rice and pasta. You can combine them with a small amount of protein and plenty of vegetables. Finish up with a piece of fruit or a small portion of a favourite dessert (try to avoid cream).

In both cases avoid alcohol at lunchtime.

Dinner

Light carbohydrate-based meals are good for the evening. If you find carbohydrates stimulating they will help ease your symptoms of depression and fatigue and allow you to feel relaxed yet focused. Moreover, if you allow yourself a light, yet satisfying, carbohydrate meal early in the evening you will be less likely to succumb to the temptation to snack or binge on sweet carbohydrates later on.

For those who find carbohydrates sedating, a light carbohydrate-based meal in the evening will allow you to relax and prepare for sleep. If, however, you have more work or activities to accomplish, or if you find you are too sleepy too early, choose a light protein meal similar to the lunchtime menu.

You may feel the need to snack during the evening. This can be alleviated by engaging in an activity which absorbs your attention and takes your mind off food. Do not totally deprive yourself, though. Why not promise yourself a small carbohydrate snack in the middle of the evening or just before bed. A small glass of warm milk and a couple of biscuits last thing at night are an ideal way to relax and prepare yourself for sleep.

Looking back on your eating diary, you may be aware of a regular time of day between meals when you feel the need for nourishment. This may be purely habit, or an opportunity to take a break from work. On the other hand, it may also be a time when your brain needs certain nutrients. One way to find out is to experiment: when you next feel the urge to eat in between meals, take a break instead, go outside if possible, walk about to get a change of scenery, or talk to someone for ten minutes. If, when you return to your work or activity, you still feel unrefreshed, lacking in energy or unable to concentrate it may be because you need to eat. Many SAD sufferers experience a slump in energy and a craving for sweet or starchy foods in the mid-afternoon. It is thought that this may be caused by a drop in serotonin levels at this time. If you notice that you regularly feel tired and depressed, or irritable and edgy and unable to concentrate in the afternoon, it is advisable to incorporate a mid-afternoon carbohydrate snack into your eating programme. The snack does not have to be big, 1 to 1.5oz (40g) is generally sufficient to restore energy and focus concentration. If you are afraid of putting on weight, why not substitute your evening dessert for an afternoon snack. Below are some suggestions for snacks:

1 slice of bread, muffin or teacake with low fat spread and sugar-free jam or honey
1 muesli bar or flapjack
1 wholemeal scone with low fat spread and sugar-free jam
2 high fibre digestive biscuits

Some people fear that by increasing their carbohydrate intake they will put on weight. This depends on the type of carbohydrate you eat. Simple carbohydrates, such as refined, sugary sweets, cakes, syrups and ice-cream are devoid of vitamins, minerals and fibre. They require little digestion and are easily assimilated into the body where they quickly raise blood sugar levels and bring a burst of energy. However, the effect is short-lived. Soon your energy level will drop and you will need another sugar infusion. Eating these carbohydrates on a regular basis puts pressure on the body which is forced to cope with the constant rise and fall of sugar levels in the body. This can lead to blood sugar disorders, such as hypoglycaemia, which also brings symptoms of depression, fatigue and confusion.

Unrefined, complex carbohydrates, such as those made from wholemeal grains (brown bread, pasta and rice), are much more health giving. Firstly, they provide essential vitamins, minerals and fibre. Secondly, they are digested and metabolized more slowly than simple sugary carbohydrates and this process burns more calories. Consequently, you will put on less weight eating complex carbohydrates than you will eating simple carbohydrates. Complex carbohydrates release a slow, steady stream of sugar into the bloodstream which maintains energy over a longer period and avoids the rapid stressful rise and fall of blood sugar levels associated with eating simple refined carbohydrates. Finally, complex carbohydrates are more satisfying when you are hungry, and provide the body with ample roughage to aid digestion and elimination.

EATING FOR DEPRESSION

The breakfast and lunchtime suggestions above provide a balanced intake of nutrients for maximum brain activity throughout the day. By keeping food light and non-fatty, minimum energy will be spent on digestion and calorific intake will be reduced. However, in winter there may be times when you need to supplement your diet with more sugary and/or starchy foods than are outlined in our suggestions above. The times you feel depressed and tired may be the moments when such foods are most called for. The temptation on these occasions is to binge, stuffing whatever comes to hand as fast as you can, until either the food runs out or you feel too ill or too guilty to go on. While this method will probably provide you with ample carbohydrate to restore depleted serotonin levels and thus lift depression and fatigue, it does a lot of damage both to your waistline and to your morale.

Curing the Crisis

An alternative to binging is to keep in store a number of low fat carbohydrate foods which you can eat in small quantities when you have a craving. The amount of carbohydrate needed to restore serotonin flow to the brain is approximately 1.5oz (4g). However, the effect will not be felt immediately. Just as a drug or medicine takes time to take effect, so carbohydrate will take time to work its way through your system to exert its effect on the brain. The best way to obtain quick relief from carbohydrate craving is to eat a small amount slowly. Here are some suggestions as to how to achieve this and avoid binging:

- Choose a favourite snack, put a small amount, about 2oz (50 gms), on a plate and go into a different room where you can sit and appreciate it to its full. Having a drink with it will accelerate assimilation into the body.
- Eat and drink slowly, and while doing so try to assess your mood, just as you did when writing down your feelings in the eating diary. Remember the notes in the diary: after eating carbohydrate you felt calmer and less depressed, so try to imagine how you will feel after this carbohydrate snack. Do not forget that the first few mouthfuls of carbohydrate are sufficient to restore serotonin levels in the brain.
- Once you have finished eating, do a calming activity, listen to music, read a magazine, watch the television, take a bath or shower, or talk to someone. This will prepare you for a more relaxed and focused mood.

If you are inclined to have slumps in the morning or during working hours, arm yourself with small 'emergency' complex carbohydrate snacks to combat fatigue, depression or cravings.

HEALTHY EATING

Concentrating on the type, quantity and timing of food intake is important for any SAD sufferer wishing to control mood and energy level. However, your eating programme should also take into account food quality. Getting ample vitamins, minerals and dietary fibre is important in maintaining general health and immunity. SAD sufferers are often prone to common winter infections and viruses because their immunity is impaired. Hence the body becomes even weaker and less able to combat the symptoms of SAD. Below are some guidelines for healthy eating to boost immunity in winter:

- Eat regular meals.
- Incorporate plenty of fresh vegetables and fruit into your diet. Some of these should be eaten raw.
- Avoid refined foods, such as white sugar, flour, rice and pasta.
- Eat wholemeal carbohydrates, such as wholemeal bread, pasta, and rice.
- Try to keep fats to a minimum.
- Eat lean meats.
- Try to occasionally eat pulses, soya or fish, rather than meat.
- Try to drink mineral water, sugar-free soft drinks and herbal teas rather than alcohol, caffeine (coffee, tea and cola) and sugar-based drinks (soda, lemonade).

ACCEPT WEIGHT GAIN

If you adopt the dietary advice given so far, your weight will be less likely to soar in the winter. However, do not forget that the population as a whole experiences an increase in appetite during the winter months, which always leads to weight gain of some degree. This is something which has to be accepted and accounted for. It happens to all of us to some extent and is probably a natural reaction which allows us to maintain energy and warmth during the cold period.

For this reason, winter is not the time to deprive yourself of food or embark on crash diets. It is a time to save energy, not to fritter it on hopeless attempts to lose weight which only end in frustration and guilt. It is vital during the winter that you direct energy at efforts to restore and maintain a balanced state of mind. Once this is achieved, your eating habits and weight gain will not assume such importance.

Most SAD sufferers know that their weight will increase in the winter. They also know that this is a temporary gain and when the spring comes the pounds will be shed and eating habits will return to normal. So, if you can accept and adapt to the transition in weight and shape which winter brings, the syndrome will not be so difficult to bear.

One of the ways of accepting weight gain throughout the winter is to ensure you feel comfortable in your clothes. This probably means that your winter wear has to be one or two sizes bigger than your summer wear. Wearing tight clothing will only be uncomfortable, and will emphasize your transition from summer to winter weight, making it more difficult to accept.

Here Are Some Tips:

- Clear your wardrobe of clothes which do not fit. Put them away until the spring.
- Make sure you have several outfits which you can comfortably wear when you are at your heaviest.
- Opt for clothing which can be adapted to fluctuations in weight, such as those with elasticated tops, or belts which can be drawn in or let out.
- When shopping do not look at the size label, but rather at the cut and style of the garment to assess if it will fit.
- Always try clothes on before purchase, or buy from shops which will refund returned goods.

Once you feel more comfortable with your body as it is, the obsession with losing weight will diminish. Instead, you can divert your attention to following the eating programme outlined in this chapter. You can adopt healthy and suitable dietary habits which will, in themselves, keep weight gain to a minimum, without depriving you of the essential foods you need during the winter months.

13

Regulating Sleep

Most SAD sufferers complain of feeling tired all the time. This symptom can easily become a vicious cycle, as daytime fatigue leads to inactivity and sporadic napping which, in turn, results in disturbed and unrefreshing night sleep, and consequently even greater fatigue the next day. The only solution to this problem is to break the cycle and establish regular sleep patterns which will accustom you to sleeping only at designated times. This will bring more refreshing night time sleep, and help alleviate daytime drowsiness.

This chapter will allow you to assess your winter sleep requirements and establish a regular sleep routine. By carrying out the exercises we suggest you will find you sleep better, wake more refreshed and feel less drowsy during the day. This will give you more energy to carry you through the winter.

ASSESS YOUR SLEEP REQUIREMENT

The first step in establishing a regular sleeping pattern is to assess your sleep needs. You can do this by keeping a record of the amount of sleep you get in each 24-hour period over a fortnight. In your diary, try to keep a record of the time you go to sleep and the time you wake up. Also make a note of any daytime or evening naps or snoozes. Only record the times you are actually asleep, not resting. Use this questionnaire to help you.

- What time did I go to bed?
- Did I go straight to sleep?
- How much time passed before I'd turned out the light?
- Did I sleep through the night?
- If not, how often did I wake up?
- What time did I wake up in the morning?
- How many hours did I sleep?
- Did I get up, or stay in bed resting, or go back to sleep?
- How did I spend the morning?
- How did I spend the afternoon?
- How did I spend the evening?

If you live with another person, you may find it helpful if they assist you in this exercise. It is not always easy to know exactly what time you fall asleep.

Add up the total number of hours slept in each 24-hour period. You will see a pattern which indicates what your average sleep time is. Now assess if this sleep time is adequate for you. Consider these questions when making your assessment.

- Do you need to be woken up by an alarm or other source?
- Do you sleep through the alarm?
- Do you continue to doze and find it hard to get up?
- Do you drop off easily in front of the television, when reading or during concerts, films, or meetings?
- Do you feel a strong urge to sleep during the day?

If your answer is yes to at least three of these questions it is likely you require more sleep. On average, SAD sufferers need approximately two hours more sleep in summer than winter. Sub-syndromal SAD sufferers often need between 30 minutes and one hour more than usual. Try adding one hour to your night time sleep every night for one month. This will usually mean going to bed an hour earlier. Note in your diary the effect on your energy/fatigue levels during the day.

Your fatigue could be due to insufficient hours of sleep, in which case adding an extra hour will be beneficial. It could also result from a disturbed sleep routine. Although you seem to be sleeping a lot, your sleep is haphazard. For example, you nap during the day or evening, then find it impossible to sleep at night. Whatever the cause of your fatigue may be, it is important to establish a regular sleep routine which will first ensure you get enough sleep and secondly determine when you sleep.

ESTABLISH A SLEEP ROUTINE

Now look at how you are going to incorporate the number of hours sleep you need into each 24-hour period. Consider these points:

- What time will you go to bed?
- What time will you wake up?
- Will you take a nap(s) during the day? If so, at what time and for how long?

It is easy to be overambitious when planning time, and often night sleep gets neglected for other more urgent or interesting activities. However, once you have established a routine, stick to it for at least one month; otherwise you will not be able to tell whether it is effective. This means sleeping for the time allocated, and not succumbing to sleep at times outside the sleep schedule. The aim of this exercise is to keep you awake, as well as ensuring you get sufficient sleep.

Pay attention to the effect of your sleep routine on the quality of your sleep and your levels of energy/fatigue during the day. You may find by the end of the month that the routine suits you and wish to continue it. If you find that you are still drowsy and tired during the day you may have to allow more night time sleep, or think about incorporating a daytime nap into your routine.

TAKING NAPS

Many people find naps productive. Winston Churchill, for example, always took an hour's nap in the afternoon which allowed him 'to press a day and a half's work into one.' Salvador Dali devised an ingenious napping technique: he would sit on a chair with a tin plate on the floor beside him. Holding a spoon over the plate he would allow himself to drift off to sleep. Of course as soon as he fell asleep the spoon clattered to the plate below, waking him up. Dali claimed a few seconds nap was enough to refresh him.

If you are suffering from severe SAD symptoms, you will probably be accustomed to dozing off during the afternoon or evening. Naps can be beneficial if your daily schedule permits, but they should form part of your sleep routine. Dozing off and on all day is not a good idea: this will leave you feeling constantly drowsy and will also prevent you from sleeping well at night. But incorporating an afternoon nap into your sleep routine may help give you the extra sleep you need, boost your energy at a time when you are beginning to flag, and help keep you going for the rest of the day. Here are a few napping rules:

- Decide on a required nap time, between 30 minutes to 1 hour, not more.
- Try to take your nap at the same time each day.
- Go to bed to nap, don't just doze off in an armchair.
- Set an alarm so that you wake after the required nap time and get up.

KEEP TO YOUR ROUTINE

Sticking to your sleep routine requires a double effort:

1 You have to keep awake at times when you may feel tired and would much rather doze or sleep.

2 You have to sleep at times when you may feel restless or unable to do so.

Although the first few weeks may be difficult, remember that it is only by establishing a sleep routine that you will finally get more and better quality sleep, and feel more refreshed and less drowsy during the day.

KEEP AWAKE

Once you have chosen the times when you sleep, you can then organize the rest of your activities around them. This will probably involve adapting your lifestyle somewhat in winter, to allow you to get the required amount of sleep and to prevent you dropping off before the allotted time.

Waking Up

The golden rule here is wake up and get up. Some say that lingering in bed half-awake and half-asleep leads to a hangover-like symptom which will remain with you the rest of the day. Getting up immediately, however cruel it may seem to the system, will ultimately make you feel better.

Having a warm shower or bath immediately on rising will help to wake you up, especially if you immerse your head. If you can bear it, follow this by a quick cold shower, it will really get you going!

You may find you want to take light therapy first thing in the morning. Some SAD sufferers have the lights next to the bed and switch them on the moment they wake. Others go to a different room for the therapy. Early morning light therapy is thought to be the most effective, and in most cases will perk you up. However, if you do it in bed, take care not to fall asleep again, try to read a book, watch television, or listen to the radio while the light box is on.

During the Day

Try to pace your day according to your energy level. If you have more energy in the morning, do important or demanding tasks then. Leave less demanding work for the afternoon if that is when you feel drowsy.

The Evening

This is usually the time when SAD symptoms are at their worst, so you will probably feel the most tired. Time your evening meal so that you allow yourself at least an hour after eating before going to bed. Once the meal is over try to engage in an active yet unstrenuous pastime. Watching television is too passive and you may fall asleep. If you find you are too tired to read, you should try to play a game, talk to someone, go for a walk, or do some gentle housework. If you arrange to see a friend, ensure that you tell them you must be in bed by the allocated time.

GETTING A GOOD NIGHT'S SLEEP

You may find at first that on getting to bed you feel agitated and unable to sleep. Planning the evening should be a subtle combination of activities which keep you awake, but also prepare you for sleep. If you engage in a gentle activity before bedtime this will help you to switch off from the day and prepare you for the night's sleep. Try to set aside problems and concerns. Avoid violence or conflict. Have a warm bath before you get into bed or read a book or magazine.

Ensure Comfortable Sleeping Conditions

Make sure your sleeping conditions are as comfortable as possible. This does not refer only to the design of the bed.

Think also about the temperature and atmosphere of the room. Sleeping in high temperatures leads to restless sleep. It is better to keep the temperature slightly low and use more bed covers, than too high. The optimum temperature for most people is between 13 and 15 degrees C (55 to 60 degrees F). For children or the elderly it should be slightly higher. It is also important to have adequate fresh air in the bedroom, so if you have a window that does not provide a draught, leave it open. Alternatively, make sure you air the bedroom well during the day. If you find that your partner disturbs your sleep or vice versa, it may be advisable to sleep apart until your sleep routine is established.

Problem Solving before You Sleep

Lying asleep and worrying over unfinished tasks, work load, unpleasant happenings during the day, guilt or inadequacies will certainly not result in restful sleep. If such thoughts persist, try to solve or alleviate them by putting the light on and writing them down. Then promise yourself the opportunity to think about them in the morning (when they will no doubt seem less important). Doing some of the exercises in Chapter Eleven may also help to put your mind at rest. If you are worried about things which need doing, make a list of priorities ready for the morning. The action of writing down your thoughts will bring them into perspective, and transfer them from your mind to paper allowing you to forget them for the time being.

Eating and Drinking

Certain foods and drinks are known to promote or inhibit sleep. The most talked of is caffeine in tea, coffee or cola drinks. As a stimulant, caffeine has a peak effect two to four hours after it is consumed. If you have sleeping problems it is probably best to avoid these drinks with or after your evening meal. The caffeine can prevent you from dropping off or may even cause you to awaken during the night. Try alternative drinks such as chicory or herb teas: chamomile tea is particularly good in aiding relaxation and helping digestion.

The nicotine in tobacco is a stimulant, hence smoking in the evening may lead to a disturbed sleep. Alcohol consumed with the evening meal or afterwards will probably make you feel drowsy, thus making it more difficult to stay awake until bedtime. Moreover, alcohol will not necessarily give you a better night's sleep.

Large meals induce fatigue. This is because energy is diverted from other sources to the digestive system. Heavy, highly spiced meals may result in disturbed sleep. Try to eat your evening meal at least two hours before going to bed. Many SAD sufferers find carbohydrate foods relax the mind and relieve agitation (see Chapters Six and Twelve). A bedtime snack of biscuits and hot milk may help you to unwind.

Disturbed Sleep

You may find that you fall asleep easily, but wake in the night or early hours of the morning, unable to get back to sleep. There are several ways of approaching these sleepless periods; you can practice techniques to lull yourself back to sleep, you can use the time to rest even if you can't sleep or, if all else fails, you can use the time profitably to do other things.

Sleeplessness is often accentuated by anxiety: the worry that you will not be able to get back to sleep makes sleep even more elusive. However, do not forget that even if you cannot sleep, rest is beneficial. Sometimes if you can accept rest, rather than trying to force yourself to sleep, anxiety is alleviated and the body relaxes sufficiently to drop off.

If staying in bed does not seem to help, an exercise called Tiegal's Air Bath can sometimes be helpful: get out of bed and walk back and forth in the room for two or three minutes without engaging in any other activity, such as reading or tidying up. Then get back under the warm bedclothes in your familiar sleep position. This brief exercise may bring sufficient relaxation for rest or sleep.

For some people sleep disturbances can be profitable times to get things done. This is especially the case if you wake early. In situations such as these, you should get up and dress warmly, as your body temperature may be low. Make sure the room you are in is comfortably heated. If early awakening becomes a regular occurrence, try to incorporate a nap into your daily routine.

Sleeping Tablets

There is a growing realization that sleeping tablets only provide temporary relief for sleep problems. A course of sleeping tablets may be prescribed over a period of time to help regulate your sleep disorder, but should not provide a long term solution. This is because sleeping tablets generally solve the symptoms, not the cause of a sleeping problem. When a person stops taking them, his/her sleep may be more disturbed than before.

It is particularly dangerous to mix sleeping pills with other types of medication, unless the combination has been prescribed by a doctor. Mixing alcohol with sleeping tablets is also unwise.

If, however, you are on a course of sleeping tablets, do not stop taking them abruptly. Consult your doctor, and withdraw gradually under supervision.

14

Spring Fever

For most of us the end of winter brings an increase in energy and enthusiasm. In earlier days, it was celebrated with festivals and dances, and even today it is ushered in with a buzz of activity in the traditional annual spring clean. You, the SAD sufferer, will be particularly aware of the changing season: as winter comes to an end you will start to feel better, and it is likely that you will want to rush around doing jobs, seeing friends and planning new ventures. This spring high usually lasts for between two and four weeks, after which you settle down to your normal summer pace.

In some cases, however, the spring fever takes you higher than you realize. Although you feel euphoric, you become hypomanic without realizing it. In this state you could lose control of your actions, act out of character, and do things you would later regret. Your hyperactivity could also cause you to become exhausted and run-down without realizing it until it is too late.

Hypomania or mania can be as destructive as SAD. It is important, therefore, to be aware of the symptoms and their implications. This chapter outlines how you may feel during the transition from winter to spring. It suggests ways of coping with hypomania and using it to your advantage, so that instead of fearing your mood swings you can approach the new season with a positive and confident outlook.

RECOGNIZE THE SYMPTOMS OF MANIA

It is necessary to be aware of how hypomania may affect you. Here are some typical symptoms:

- You feel full of energy, confidence and new ideas, you feel you could take on the world.
- You talk fast, holding forth in company, you make jokes and are witty.
- You rush about doing things, you start many projects, but don't finish any of them.
- You feel irritated by anyone who does not keep up, or who tries to slow you down.
- You are disinhibited: you say things which may be embarrassing or hurtful to others without thinking.
- You have grandiose ideas about yourself and your abilities.
- You form new relationships with people you wouldn't normally get on with.
- You look for sexual excitement: a new partner or an affair.
- You go to bed late and wake early.
- You don't eat much.
- You spend lots of money, regardless of whether you can afford it.

COPING WITH HYPOMANIA

Monitor Your Actions

Hypomania is a difficult condition to control, but one of the first steps to managing it is to be aware of your symptoms. By watching your actions you can take steps to control the syndrome or, if it is serious, to seek medical help. Do not forget that during the spring you may not be yourself, your actions could hurt others and be detrimental to yourself. If you feel you are losing control do not hesitate to seek professional advice.

An excellent way of increasing your awareness of sudden changes in moods is to keep a diary. Entries do not have to be lengthy, though once you get started you may find you enjoy the act of expressing your feelings in written form. At the end of each day write brief notes about how you felt and what you did each day. You will probably find that in winter you write little because you are not doing much. As spring approaches your energy level will change and you will start to write more. At the end of each week look back over your notes. Compare them to the ones you made the week before. Look to see if you are writing more or less, or if your activities and feelings have changed. Keeping an eye on your notes will help you recognize if you are moving into a hypomanic or manic stage.

Talk to Others

If possible, prepare those who are around you on a regular basis for your change in mood and increased energy level. It can be difficult for a family member or work colleague to appreciate that someone who has been as quiet as a dormouse all winter can suddenly be full of enthusiasm, energy and ideas. Even if your hypomania seems mild to you, it will be very noticeable to the people who have seen you regularly over the winter. If they understand that this sudden mood swing is part of the SAD syndrome, they will accept it more easily.

Sharing your feelings with others has the added advantage of reducing your guilt and concern about your state. Bottling up the fear of hypomania can turn to paranoia, where you avoid people for risk of offending them or, worse still, losing control. If you explain to others what is happening this will allow you to be yourself and not constantly feel afraid to speak or act for fear of seeming abnormal.

Use Energy Productively

Try to arrange your work so that you can channel your spring energy into creative and exciting tasks. Some SAD sufferers I have interviewed found that in order to do this they had to change the nature of their work. Some became self-employed, others took jobs where they were less tied to a constant routine. Certain jobs lend themselves to more activity in spring and summer than winter. If you are working for someone, it may be appropriate to explain your summer highs and winter lows; you may find that they are prepared to accept that you may be less productive in the winter, as long as your enthusiasm and output are high in the summer.

Find a relaxing, yet engaging, pastime. This may be in the form of exercise or a hobby. Spring could be the time to start a new sport or evening class. Many people find that their creative ability is enhanced during hypomanic phases. Sketching, painting, photography or writing poetry will engage and relax the mind.

Try to occupy yourself with calming jobs around the house and garden. Tending plants or cleaning the stove, for example, are activities which will be productive, satisfying and calming.

Delay Major Changes

Often hypomania brings a sudden desire for change and excitement. You may suddenly find things in your life you want to change. Your existence seems boring, so you look for excitement in the form of a new job, a new relationship, or perhaps a move to a different location or home. While some of these changes may be necessary and positive, others may be transient desires which will pass. To avoid doing things that you may later regret, do not make any major changes for at least a month. Write down what you would like to do, so that it isn't forgotten, then when a month is up, reassess the idea.

Take Care in Relationships

Throughout the winter your desire for affection or physical contact probably decreased. As spring approaches you may suddenly experience renewed interest in sex. This change of feeling may be difficult for a partner to understand or accept. His/her feelings may have changed as a result of lack of contact or affection. It is important that partners appreciate that sexual appetite is affected by SAD, so that they do not take your lack of interest personally. Discussing how you both feel will help diffuse the tension created in such situations and bring you closer.

Do not make any impulsive decisions to end a serious relationship at this stage. Wait until a month has passed and reassess the situation.

If you decide to embark on new sexual encounters take adequate measures to protect yourself from unwanted pregnancy and/or sexually transmitted diseases.

Avoid Financial Indiscretion

After a winter of depression and withdrawal you are likely to make for the shops with enthusiasm at the first sign of spring. While you don't want to deprive yourself of this pleasure, take care what you buy and where. To avoid impulse buying, leave major purchases such as furniture, washing machines, etc, until later. For smaller items, such as clothing, take somebody along with you for a second opinion, and go to stores which give a refund if the goods are returned. Make sure you keep receipts and packaging so you can take the goods back if you decide you have bought something you don't really want or need.

If you share a joint account, it may be a good idea to establish with the other person what you have available to spend at this time. Try not to use credit cards; put them away until you are feeling more in control.

Maintain Your Energy

Although you may feel at this time that nothing can stop you, your body will eventually tire from constant activity. Moreover, you are probably sleeping and eating less, and are losing weight. All this can lead to extreme exhaustion if you do not take measures to maintain your strength through adequate nutrition and rest. You should therefore, channel some of your energy into preparing appetizing healthy meals. Buy some new cookery books and experiment. Aim for low fat recipes with high protein and fibre: poultry or fish, wholemeal bread, rice and pasta and plenty of raw vegetables. Reduce sugars and processed foods as much as possible. Drink juices, mineral water or tea, rather than coffee. Try to eat three regular meals a day, do not forget to eat, and don't skip meals just because you don't feel hungry.

Make sure you get adequate rest. Engaging in some of the activities already mentioned, such as writing, drawing and painting will help you to rest the body.

COPING WITH MANIA

The strategies described above have helped many SAD sufferers to make the most of spring. You will probably be one of those for whom the end of winter requires just a little caution. However, it is important to watch your health. If you find you are sleeping very little, or not at all, and if you are unable to eat and are rapidly losing weight, you could be suffering from an extreme reaction to spring, known as mania. This is found in about fifteen to twenty per cent of SAD sufferers and if left untreated the sheer exhaustion and rapid weight loss can be highly dangerous. If you feel you are suffering from mania (one of the first signs is not being able to sleep) do not hesitate to seek professional help.

Mania can be successfully treated with drugs. Lithium carbonate is the most commonly prescribed medication, and can bring mania in check within ten days. While waiting for the lithium carbonate to take effect many doctors prescribe a temporary major tranquillizer, such as Holoperidol or Chlorpromazine. This will control your mood until the lithium takes over. Some SAD patients take lithium carbonate on a regular basis to prevent both depression and mania, as its main action is the regulation of mood swings. However, when taking it you must have regular blood tests to ensure that you are taking the correct dose. Too much can be dangerously toxic to the body. Minor side-effects of lithium carbonate which may occur in the first two weeks of taking the drug are nausea, loose stools, increased urine and a metallic taste. Major side-effects are visible shaking, thirst, vomiting and diarrhoea, any of which should be referred immediately to your doctor.

Drugs such as these have to be treated with caution. Do not hesitate to discuss the effects with your doctor. Chapter Nine deals more fully with how to approach drug therapy for SAD.

15

Daylight Exercise

Two of the basic requirements for a healthy existence are fresh air and exercise. To this we can now add a third: natural daylight. In Chapters Five and Six we looked at the importance of light to health. It provides vital nutrients to maintain healthy bones, and it plays a significant part in regulating the biological clocks and hormonal mechanisms of the body. Above all it is the essential therapy used to alleviate the symptoms of SAD. Therefore getting out into the natural sunlight every day is a central part of this self help SAD programme.

Yet how many of us manage to get a regular dose of natural light each day? Our sedentary winters are spent cooped up in buildings with little natural daylight, which are often badly ventilated and over heated. It is no wonder we feel tired, depressed and unmotivated.

Exercise, fresh air and light are vital nutrients, just as food and water are. We would not consider going for long periods without enough to eat or drink, yet we often ignore our bodies requirements when it comes to outdoor exercise. The commonest excuses are lack of time, willpower, energy or interest. When suffering from SAD these excuses seem even more valid; your energy level and mood are low, you feel cold and anti-social, the last thing you want to do is step outside and move about. But getting natural daylight, fresh air and exercise is a highly effective way to combat SAD symptoms. No matter how bad you feel, it will make you feel better. This is why:

- Outdoor exercise provides you with increased natural daylight. However grey and dreary it may seem outside, you can be guaranteed that the light out there is of higher intensity than indoor artificial lighting. Even on a dreary day the light intensity outside is around 10,000 lux. This is the same intensity as the latest light boxes which have proven effective when used for as little as 30 minutes per day. Hence 30 minutes outside could give you the equivalent of a daily session of phototherapy. Getting outside should of course supplement your phototherapy, not replace it. However, if your symptoms are slight, as in the case of sub-syndromal SAD, you may find that getting outside regularly is an adequate way of combating them.

- Outdoor exercise provides your body with more oxygen and thus raises your energy level. Breathing fresh air is even more vital to the body than food. You can live for several weeks without food, for several days without water, but only a few minutes without air. The oxygen in air is essential for breaking down the nutrients the body receives, and converting them into energy. Therefore, the amount of oxygen you receive will have a direct impact on how much mental and physical energy you generate.

  As well as being vital to the energy mechanism, breathing fresh air also fulfils another important function. It removes carbon dioxide and wastes from the body. When we convert nutrients into energy, carbon dioxide is released as a by-product. Carbon dioxide is a poison and, if left to accumulate in the body, will gradually destroy cells. Once it is exhaled, carbon dioxide remains in the atmosphere. For this reason it is important to constantly renew the air in a building or to go outside to get fresh air. If you remain indoors with a stale air supply you inhale less oxygen, and more carbon dioxide. The result is decreased energy and a build up of toxins in the body.

- Taking exercise enhances the effects of breathing by getting more oxygen to the whole body. This is because movement of the muscles increases the flow of blood to the heart. As a result the heart pumps more vigorously and increases blood circulation, which carries more oxygen to the cells to produce more energy. Regular exercise strengthens the heart so that this process happens continuously, producing more energy even when you are not exercising. This is why, paradoxically, people who exercise regularly have more energy than those who don't. A sedentary lifestyle allows the heart to grow lazy: it pumps less blood, less oxygen is received by the cells and less energy is generated.

Many people shy away from exercise, claiming that they do not have enough time to do it. What they don't realize is that by exercising you give yourself more time because you have more energy.

• Anyone who regularly exercises outdoors will know the effect it has on mental state. It is impossible to sustain depression, anger or anxiety during and immediately after vigorous exercise. Research studies have looked at the effect of exercise on mood and stress levels. One proved that jogging for half an hour three times a week is at least as effective as psychotherapy in treating depression. Another showed that stress levels were much lower in people who regularly exercised compared with those who lead a sedentary lifestyle. The reason why exercise should lead to a change in mood is not clear; some think it is due to the fact that exercise diverts the mind and that physical exertion blocks out mental stress. Others say it could be a result of the increase of blood and oxygen reaching the brain which allows it to function better. It is also suggested that the increase in the rate of production of brain transmitters which occurs during exercise could play a role in changing mood during exercise.

• Most people look to exercise as a means of losing weight. While this should not be the sole objective of an exercise programme, there is no doubt that by increasing heart rate, and energy generation, more calories are burned and weight is reduced. In addition, regular exercise reduces appetite. This is because by keeping blood levels high it prevents the fall in blood sugar levels which can lead to sudden cravings for food, in particular carbohydrates.

- Many of the somatic aches and pains which are character-istic of SAD are relieved by gentle outdoor exercise. The blood circulation is stimulated and more oxygen and nutri-ents reach stiff muscles and joints. Exercise also stimulates a sluggish digestive system and aids efficient elimination.

- After regular exercise the body feels relaxed yet not tired, supple yet not stiff. You will breathe easier, your stamina for work will be increased and you will sleep better. A fitter and firmer body, increased energy and a more open and cheerful state of mind will dramatically raise your self-confidence and help in combating the symptoms of SAD throughout the winter.

HOW TO APPROACH OUTDOOR EXERCISE

Surprisingly little effort is required to enjoy outdoor exercise. What is definitely needed, however, is a positive attitude. Despite our knowledge that 'exercise is good for you' most of us have little enthusiasm. We see exercise as a chore, an added obligation in an already full and exhausting day. What we often forget is the enjoyment factor: the pleasure of tramping through the autumn leaves, the exhilaration of running with the wind in your face, the satisfaction of a day spent tending the garden. Not to mention the enjoyable after-effects: the glowing warmth when you come back indoors, with tingling skin and a hearty appetite and the pleasant relaxation and peace of mind which follows vigorous exercise and plentiful fresh air.

You do not have to be a marathon runner to benefit from outdoor exercise, but you do have to establish a regular routine. In order for this to succeed it is essential to find an activity which provides interest and enjoyment. Without it your efforts will not survive.

The next secret to successful exercising is not to overdo things. The body takes time to build up stamina. If you push yourself too hard at the start you will easily become exhausted and discouraged. Your routine should continue all year round so, to make it easier, begin in the summer, when you feel more energetic and ease yourself gradually into a routine, spending as little as fifteen or thirty minutes on your chosen activity. The aim is to find the optimum balance: sufficient exercise to increase your energy, but not too much which will exhaust and discourage you. Here are some ideas to get you started:

Walking

Walking is an ideal way to start exercising. It is an activity which can be practised by anyone at any time, with the minimum inconvenience. Walking can be incorporated into other everyday activities, such as shopping, or getting from a to b. Alternatively, it can be an opportunity to appreciate the countryside, visit a site of interest or get to know a town. The only investment required is enthusiasm and a comfortable pair of shoes.

Incorporate walking into your day. Make a date to spend fifteen to thirty minutes of the day walking. The best time is in the morning or early afternoon, when the light is brightest, but if this is not possible, any time is better than none at all. Try some of these ways of incorporating walking into your day.

• Get up for a walk before breakfast. The fresh air and early morning light will rid you of that groggy sleepiness and the exercise will relax your mind and energize your body, ready for the day.

- Incorporate walking into your transport plan. If possible walk rather than using the car or public transport. For short journeys you may be surprised to find that walking does not take much longer than waiting for the bus or sitting in traffic jams, and is a lot more pleasant. If you have to use the bus or train, make sure you walk to the pick up point. To extend your walk try to choose a bus stop or station which is slightly further from home. If you must use your car, make sure you park a fifteen minute walk from home or from work.

- Use local shops which you can walk to regularly, rather than taking the car to far-flung shopping centres.

- If you work, use your lunch break to go for a walk. You can eat a snack before or after going out. Or, if the weather is fine, stop on your way for a sandwich. Try to avoid busy roads, instead visit a park, garden or water spot if there is one nearby. If your walk has to take in ships or a bank, aim for those which give you at least a fifteen minute walk through quiet roads. If possible shop in outdoor markets where you will be exposed to natural light as much as possible.

- If you do not work, your walk can be timed to coincide with the hours of optimum sunlight during the morning. You also have more choice about where you walk, and can combine it with visiting a friend, or pursuing a hobby or interest, such as bird or plant spotting. If in town you could study the architecture of the buildings, or aim for a site of interest.

Often it is pleasantly relaxing to walk alone. However, if you have a friend who is interested in regular walks, going together may stimulate you to walk more often. Alternatively a dog makes an enthusiastic walking companion, and one which will certainly not let you forget your need for daily exercise.

Equip yourself for walking in all weather. If you are protected from the rain and cold there is no reason why you should not walk all year round. Wear comfortable shoes and protective clothing which can withstand the wet, and keep an umbrella with you. Make sure you are warm enough: a hat can be a great comfort on a cold and windy winter's day.

Choose walks with some inclines and set a fairly brisk pace. Your walk should make you a little out of breath. After the first two weeks, increase your walk time by another 10-15 minutes. If you are restricted by working hours, incorporate another walk at another time of day. After six weeks, monitor how you are walking: you will probably find that your pace has increased and that you are covering more ground in less time. In this case you can extend your walk or, if you feel up to it, substitute it for a gentle run.

Walking is the first stage in your outdoor exercise programme and one that can easily be incorporated into your everyday schedule. Once you are into the swing of walking regularly your energy will increase and you may want to look for a further outdoor sport or hobby which can be practised once or twice a week. Here are some suggestions:

Sports and Recreation

The boom in fitness and health in the last twenty years has provided a wide range of classes and facilities for exercise. When you are choosing what to do, look for sports or recreational activities in which you are already skilled or wish to become skilled. You are more likely to pursue something on a regular basis if you are competent at it or really keen to learn. Think back to any activities you enjoyed in the past, or look to ones which you have always wanted to try. Perhaps now is your chance.

Take the following into consideration:

- How much time can you spend per week on this activity?
- Where can you do it?
- What equipment do you need?
- How much will it cost you to carry out the activity?
- Will you do it alone or with others?

Exercise in which your body constantly uses oxygen is considered to be the best for overall fitness. Also known as aerobic exercise, these sports maintain a rhythmical movement which raises your heart beat and increases oxygen intake. Running, swimming, cycling, cross-country skiing, fast walking, rope skipping and dancing are all examples of aerobic exercise.

If you are not used to exercising or have any kind of heart condition or high blood pressure and are over 40, it is advisable to have a check-up before engaging in vigorous aerobic exercise. In the majority of cases there is no reason why you will not be able to partake, whatever your age, providing you pace yourself properly, by starting gently and building up time and intensity gradually. Swimming and cycling are good aerobic activities to start with if you are unused to exercising. Although swimming does not always get you outside, it has the advantage of exercising all body muscles and the immersion in water has a wonderfully relaxing effect.

If aerobic exercise does not appeal, there are plenty of other activities which get you out in the fresh air and sunlight and provide the opportunity for movement. While these might not get the heart beating as fast as does aerobic exercise, they do provide the opportunity for constant mobility, which stretches muscles and loosens joints. Think about the bending and stretching endured by serious gardeners, sailing enthusiasts and golfers. Such activities still bring increased blood and oxygen to the brain and body. In addition they provide diversion and interest which are as important as physical exercise.

ESTABLISH A ROUTINE

- Decide when you will carry out your activity. Set aside a regular time and place for exercise and make these part of your regular schedule.
- Set your goals, ie how far you will run, or for how long you will garden and what your tasks will be. Remember this is not a crash programme. Avoid the tendency to make up for years of inactivity in a few weeks.
- Warm up and cool down with gentle movements before and after exercise. This is particularly important for aerobic exercise and any activity which involves stretching. Walking for five or ten minutes before and after exercise is a good way to limber up.

Here is an example of a SAD sufferer who successfully combined exercise with phototherapy to combat SAD:

JO

I used to be a buying controller in the fashion industry. I travelled all over the world with my job. However, about six years ago I started to find that in the winter I had to drag myself out of bed in the mornings. I used to spend the whole week forcing myself to do what had once been an enjoyable and stimulating job. On Friday night I would get home and go straight to bed, where I would stay until Monday morning. It was the only way I could get my strength back to start another week. I managed to just about control my mood at work, but I was extremely bad-tempered at home. I was nasty and accusing to my husband and children. I wasn't myself at all. I didn't want to be bothered with anything: cooking, ironing and shopping were abandoned, even my beautiful window boxes died, I just couldn't be bothered to water them.

I am now retired. I use light therapy regularly to control

SAD, but I complement it with swimming and gardening. I get up at around 5 or 5.30 a.m. and use the light box for two hours. I then go to a local leisure centre and, depending on how I feel, I swim for between thirty minutes and one hour. I swim slowly, using the old-fashioned side stroke. I generally do on average about fifty lengths of the 45ft pool.

I find this routine very beneficial in several ways: it helps discipline me to get up in the morning, and it relaxes me. When you have SAD it is very difficult to discipline yourself to do anything. You feel so exhausted, that you can't motivate yourself. Before I started exercising, I used to find that by the autumn I would feel so bad that I wanted to stay in bed all day, I couldn't even drag myself out to get in the shower. I am now convinced that light therapy and swimming have been the most effective treatment for me. Now I know how the swim will benefit me I am motivated to get up in the morning to do my light therapy and to be exercising by 7.30 a.m. Some people think I'm stupid getting up so early, but it's worth making the effort for the relaxation it gives me. SAD is a stressful illness, and by swimming I can relieve myself of anxiety and relax. It sets me up for the day.

LIGHT ACTIVE HOLIDAYS

Many SAD sufferers tend to take winter holidays rather than summer ones. They find that their symptoms are relieved on visiting a warm, sunny location, which has a longer photoperiod than their home town. Some also opt for winter sports. They find the bright sunshine and reflection of intense light off the white snowy surroundings makes up for the shortened day. Going on holiday in winter will not cure SAD, but it may relieve your symptoms temporarily and, if you choose the right type of holiday, it may provide you with some much needed relaxation.

People in the northern hemisphere often find February is

the worst month for SAD. In the southern hemisphere it is usually July. If you decide to plan a holiday this could be the time to choose.

Opt for locations which have a low latitude. If you are in the northern hemisphere head as far south as you can afford to go. For Europeans, the south of Spain, Italy, Greece or north Africa are good locations. If you are in north America or Canada you may choose to head to southern California, Miami, Central or South America. If you are in the southern hemisphere aim as far north as you can, to northern Australia, New Caledonia, Malaysia or Indonesia. The map and chart in Chapter Two will help you to establish the areas which are nearest to the equator, these are the areas in which the incidence of SAD is low or non-existent.

If you go to a sunny, warm area you will, of course, spend more time outside, thus benefiting from light, fresh air, and perhaps, exercise. Winter sports, usually held in mountainous areas, will bring exhilarating air, beautiful scenery and plenty of diversion and exercise, though not necessarily a longer photoperiod.

When planning a winter holiday it is important to take your own tastes into account. There is no point in going to a place you dislike, just because the days are longer and brighter. You will end up bored and disappointed. It is equally important to find a place where there are activities, local culture and sites of interest which stimulate you and allow you to relax and forget your symptoms.

Do not place too many hopes on a winter holiday. Some SAD sufferers I interviewed have waited in anticipation for a holiday which they thought would cure their illness. They were bitterly disappointed and found it even more difficult to cope with the symptoms while they were away than when at home. Perhaps the sunlight was not strong enough to relieve their symptoms, perhaps the stress of being away from home while they were ill was too much to cope with. Don't forget, travelling is a tiring occupation and your body may not be able to handle the disruption.

Some people suffer a slight attack of hypomania or mania when they suddenly relocate to a bright area. The symptoms of mania and how to cope with them are listed in Chapter Four. Make sure you watch your actions and behaviour while you are away to be aware of any rapid mood swings.

Some SAD sufferers report that the return home to grey skies brings them down with a bump after an enjoyable holiday. After three or four days of being home their symptoms are as bad as before. Unfortunately this is the nature of SAD. You need constant light to keep symptoms at bay, so do not expect to come home from holiday cured. Be prepared to start light therapy and your self help techniques again.

MOVING HOME

I have come across a small number of SAD sufferers who found the relief of being in a location of lower latitude persuaded them to move there permanently. While this seems the obvious solution to SAD, it is not the easiest choice for most of us. Unlike birds who migrate each year, humans have responsibilities, families, jobs, houses, cultural ties, all of which can make moving to a different town, country or state difficult. However if you are in a position to relocate, it is advisable to test out the location before making a permanent move. Try to spend at least three winters there, to make sure it will provide the relief you are seeking. Make quite sure it has the length of photoperiod you require to lift symptoms. Weigh up the advantages and disadvantages of relocation compared with those of staying where you are and treating your condition with light therapy. And above all, do not make any rash decisions.

16

The Indoor Environment

Despite our best efforts to get outside and receive natural sunlight, most of us spend a large proportion of our time inside during the winter months. Our surroundings inevitably influence our mood and physical state. For this reason it is important that the atmosphere and conditions at home and at work are comfortable and conducive to health. For SAD sufferers this means bringing as much light as possible inside, in order to create a pleasant, spring-like refuge in which to escape the dreary winter months.

Light can be brought into the indoor environment in a number of different ways, depending on your location and situation. You may decide that you want to make major changes to the entire living or working space. If this is not feasible you could equally benefit from making minor inexpensive alterations to a single room or personal space. These are some of the things we will consider:

- how to make the most of existing natural sources of light
- how to add new sources of natural light by restructuring
- what to look for in the ideal home or workplace
- how to introduce light by redecorating
- how to brighten up the indoor environment with colourful accessories
- how to make the most of artificial lighting

As you will see it is not just light which influences mood and well-being. This chapter will also look at how temperature and atmosphere can contribute to producing a pleasant and relaxing indoor environment.

MAKING THE MOST OF EXISTING LIGHT

Although modern buildings are not always designed to maximize natural light, there are methods which can be employed to encourage light into your indoor environment. Here are some simple and inexpensive ideas:

- Assess where the light enters your building. Are you making the most of it? There is no point in having a sun-flooded lounge if you are shut away in a dark study on the other side of the house. Try to make use of the rooms which have the most winter light.
- Place chairs for reading, desks or worktops near the window, where they will gain maximum benefit from natural light. Built-in window seats are perfect places to sit.
- Use light-coloured paints on the areas around, below and outside windows. This will reflect light into the building.
- Ensure that plants, shrubs and creepers are not obscuring windows.
- Keep the windows clean.
- Ensure that the curtains are drawn right back, on a track which clears the window panes. Avoid net curtains or blinds which obscure the light.
- Never allow a piece of furniture to obscure a window.
- Do not clutter window sills with books, objects or plants.

Most of these measures are easy to implement and are not permanent. Therefore, if you live in an environment where you wish to maximize on light intake during the winter, yet minimize its entry in the hot summer, the use of blinds, curtains and deciduous plants to obscure windows throughout the summer months will be possible.

ADAPTING AN EXISTING BUILDING

There are many exciting and exotic ways of introducing light into a building or room if you are prepared and able to do major alterations. You may imagine a dream conservatory where you and your plants can bask in the sun. You may have wide sophisticated French windows in mind. On a more modest scale, it can be surprisingly inexpensive to transform a small, dingy upstairs room into a pool of sunlight by incorporating a skylight. When considering restructuring, remember these points:

- If possible, extend the height of the window, rather than the width, in this way more sky and light is gained.
- The higher the window the more light will enter. Adding skylights is an effective way of introducing maximum light.

Before embarking on major alterations, think about how you will use the room and how it will be furnished. For example, if it is to be a study or work room, make sure that the light will fall in the position where you will be working, where there is room for a worktop or desk. Remember that increased window space lets out more heat. If you are considering a large expanse of window, will you be able to cover the added heating expenses? Double glazing, insulation and draughtproofing will, of course, preserve energy and help keep heating costs down.

A popular conversion which is being made in houses today is the addition of a conservatory onto an existing building. This is basically a room built onto the sun-facing side of the building, made up in part of a large expanse of glass to allow through as much light and heat from the sun as possible.

MOVING TO A NEW ENVIRONMENT

It is surprising how much time, money and effort people spend on creating beautiful homes and offices, but how little attention they give to lighting. Today, homes are usually chosen by virtue of their size and economy. Their proximity to public services or the workplace are generally considered more important than their position in relation to the sun. Some SAD sufferers notice that a move to a dark, artificially-lit office or home makes their symptoms worse. Moving to an environment which receives more natural light often helps alleviate symptoms. If you suffer from SAD in its mild or acute form, access to natural daylight should be one of the considerations on your list when searching out a new location. Here are some points to think about:

- What is the position of the building in terms of orientation to the sun? For maximum daylight the house should face south in the northern hemisphere, and north in the southern hemisphere.
- Does anything obstruct the sunlight, in particular during the winter? Deciduous trees may provide welcome shade in the summer and allow sunlight through in the winter. Evergreens, on the other hand will block light all year round.
- How big are the windows?
- Can you see ways in which you could affordably adapt the building to incorporate more light?

When looking over a building (house, office, work space or apartment) with a view to buying or renting, it is important to see it during the day. Observe if the present habitants have the lights on to show the rooms. Ask to see it without artificial lighting. You will soon get an impression of how much natural light it receives. Consider in which rooms you will spend most of your time. It's no good having a sunflooded bedroom if you spend most of your time in the west-facing kitchen. Rooms positioned within a thirty degree angle either east or west of due south (north in the southern hemisphere) all get good midday sun. Rooms facing east get the morning sun, while those facing west will be cooler and darker during most of the winter.

INTERIOR DECORATION

Many SAD sufferers have found that a little effort in redecorating can make a big difference to the amount of light and the atmosphere of a room. Decorating is not something you will want to do in the winter, but it is something worth bearing in mind when spring comes along and your energy is increased.

The quality of light in a building or room does not depend solely on the position and the size and quantity of light inlets. Interior decoration and colour schemes are also important. Light reflects off walls, ceilings and objects in varying

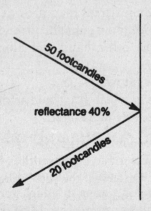

The quantity of light which bounces back off surfaces is known as reflectance.

degrees, depending on their tone and texture. The amount of light which bounces off a surface is known as 'reflectance' and is expressed as a percentage. For example, the reflectance level of white or cream walls is between sixty and seventy per cent, which means that over half the light that shines on them is reflected back. More sombre hues have a much lower reflectance percentage and thus make the room darker.

Light coloured walls tend to make rooms look brighter and larger. Bold paints or heavily patterned walls have the opposite effect, and are often used to reduce the apparent height of a room or to produce a more confined, intimate atmosphere.

There is a wide variety of white or off-white shades to choose from when decorating. While you want your environment to be light, beware of making the colour scheme so pale that the room appears cold and uninviting. Off-white shades such as magnolias, peaches and creams are not as stark as pure white, yet still have high reflectance. Don't forget, if you choose a pale shade or white as your basic colour its coolness can be offset by colourful curtains, furniture and accessories to add warmth.

If you are unable to redecorate and change the basic colour scheme, try to introduce light accessories into the room. Light coloured wall hangings or pictures, a light rug (light is reflected from the floor as well as the walls and ceilings), light coloured furniture covers and curtains. Abundant use of mirrors will reflect more light and give a feeling of space.

ADDING COLOUR AND TEXTURE

SAD sufferers have found it important to plan colour schemes, especially for rooms in which they spend a lot of time. Your basic colour scheme should be one which encourages light into the room. How you use colour to add atmosphere to the indoor environment is a personal matter, though, and one which you can use to your advantage to influence your mood. Colour is intricately linked to associations and feelings: it can make us feel warm and comfortable or cold and gloomy. 'Feeling blue' or 'seeing red' are not pure idiosyncracies of language, but refer to the psychological power of colour in our lives.

The ancient cultures of China, India and Egypt used colour to influence mood and even to heal illness. In Chinese medicine, colours are divided up between yin and yang; colours from the red end of the spectrum, such as gold, yellow and orange are said to be energizing yang colours, while blues and violets are cool, reserved yin colours; green in Chinese tradition is considered neutral. Modern psychologists have determined the moods which people associate with the colours of the spectrum. They found that warm colours such as red, orange and yellow are the most energizing and exciting, while cooler colours, such as green blue, and earth colours are more tranquillizing. Such observations have been put to use with much success in fashion, marketing and advertising.

Schools, hospitals and offices have also benefited from the knowledge that colour can induce relaxation or stimulate production. You can use the same techniques in your home or workplace to create an atmosphere which will help lift your mood and energy level. When choosing accessories to brighten up your room consider the psychological associations of the following colours.

red = warmth, energy, stimulation, excitement
orange/yellow = joy, liveliness, youth, intellect
pink = love, nurturing
green = freshness, harmony
blue/grey = distant, restful, cool
beige/brown = conservative, safe, earthy

Of course, the hue of each colour and how it is blended with other shades will influence the overall psychological impact.

Think about the warm reds, golds and pinks which come from natural wood, plaster, brick, stone and fibre. These colours add warmth and texture to a room, while keeping it simple. A variety of textures (a shiny polished wooden table or a rough plastered fireplace, for example) adds different concentrations of light reflection, shadows and interest to the atmosphere. You are less likely to tire of subtle natural colours than of synthetic dyes. The addition of greenery provided by plants will introduce a sense of freshness and harmony to any room. Experiment with inexpensive items such as cushion covers, vases, even fresh flowers, to add flashes of colour to the room. These can be changed according to your mood and the season.

MAKING THE MOST OF ARTIFICIAL LIGHTING

The shortened daylight hours and long evenings of winter make it essential to supplement natural light with artificial sources. The type of lighting chosen and the way it is arranged influences the overall decor and atmosphere, not to mention our mood and health. Both your home and your workplace can almost certainly benefit from a rearrangement of and additions to their lighting.

Most interior design magazines and books advocate standard incandescent lighting to achieve a relaxed, informal atmosphere and show examples of cosy, golden, romantic rooms. However, while highly atmospheric, these interiors are a disaster for the SAD sufferer for whom dim, yellow light only serves to emphasize the semi-darkness which shrouds us for most of the winter. As we saw in Chapter Five, the intensity and quality of artificial light affects activity levels and mood. Incandescent bulbs produce low intensity light from the red end of the spectrum, which is conducive to relaxation and sleep; brighter blue-green cool fluorescent light is more activating, while full spectrum light is the closest to that of natural daylight. When choosing the lighting for your home or workplace, bear in mind the atmosphere you wish to achieve in a room and what you want to do there. If you plan to spend a lot of time in a room or be active, for example, in an office or kitchen, try to install a lighting scheme which approximates natural daylight as far as possible.

To do this your basic options are to install cool white fluorescent or full spectrum lighting. The advantages and disadvantages of each are outlined below.

Fluorescent Lighting

Cheap to install and to run, fluorescent lighting is five times more energy efficient than incandescent bulbs. However, some people find it produces an uncomfortable glare, which can result in headaches and eye strain. These complaints are generally due to inadequate installation and low quality bulbs and fixtures. It is best to opt for quality fluorescent lighting, such as cool white deluxe or phosphor lamps, and make sure the bulbs are protected by a plastic or glass diffuser.

If you do not wish to install overhead lighting, mini compact fluorescent lamps are available which can be screwed into an incandescent fixture.

Full Spectrum Lighting

The nearest to natural light in terms of colours emitted, this lighting is often more popular than the blue white light of fluorescents. Full spectrum lighting provides thirty per cent less glare than fluorescent and is more comfortable on the eyes. Because the light is very similar to that of daylight, the colours seen under it are more accurate than those seen under fluorescent or incandescent light. This explains its popularity with designers and artists who need to identify colours and detail with precision. (Madame Tussaud's waxwork makers swear by it). It has also been shown to increase visual acuity and concentration (see Chapter Five.) Full spectrum lighting comes in the form of plain or twist tubes of varying lengths, which are fitted into standard fluorescent overhead fittings. It is about five times more expensive than standard fluorescent lighting, but lasts longer, and generally has an eighteen month warranty. The tubes emit a small percentage of ultra violet, which, as we saw in Chapter Five, provides the body with vitamin D. If you do not wish to install overhead linear lamps, you may prefer adjustable full spectrum desk lamps (for availability consult the Resources section at the back of this book).

An advantage of linear lamps is that several can be placed together to increase intensity of light. A disadvantage is that the light they produce is flat and shadowless. You can over-come this lack of variety in light by incorporating warm colours and contrasting textures into the decor, along with supplementary light sources. If the room is multipurpose, for example a kitchen-diner, you may wish to install full spec-trum or fluorescent lighting for cooking and preparation, but also have a few spot incandescents in the eating area to provide a more relaxed eating atmosphere.

Although excellent for general household or office use, none of the lamps generally used in the home or the office provide the intensity of light necessary to treat SAD (that is light of at least 2,500 lux), and should not be used to do so. However, many SAD sufferers and especially those with sub-syndromal symptoms find that a general increase in light quality in the home and workplace helps contribute to keeping symptoms at bay.

For rooms where a softer atmosphere is desired, such as the sitting room, bedroom or dining room, incandescent bulbs may be more suitable and flexible. Here you can replace standard bulbs for neodymium lamps which filter out the yellow rays and emit a white light. Using high wattage neodymium lamps in different locations around the room will give a bright yet versatile, light. Do not rely on a single central overhead fixture. Instead distribute light sources around the room with the help of spotlights, wall fittings, table and standing lamps.

For maximum brightness, regularly dust light bulbs, shades and fittings. The average life of an incandescent bulb is between 750 and 1,000 hours (around 45 days of continuous use), after which the light emitted dwindles. Fluorescent bulbs should be replaced after 7,000 hours (around ten months of continuous use). Flickering fluorescent lights can be dangerous and uncomfortable to the eyes and should be immediately replaced. Full spectrum bulbs have a life span of 20,000 hours and an eighteen month warranty.

Choosing Shades

When choosing a lamp shade take the shape and amount of light it will cast into consideration. Full spectrum lighting is generally used without shades, in order to prevent distortion of the colour spectrum. The lamps can however be camouflaged by beams, cornices or valances. With fluorescent lighting it is preferable to cover the bare bulb with a screening or shielding device, usually a clear plastic or glass diffuser. Lampshades for mini fluorescents, neodymium or incandescent bulbs can throw direct light downwards and upwards through the shade openings, so these should be as wide as possible. The openings allow light to reflect back off the walls, floor and ceiling. The amount of light which is diffused sideways depends on the transparency of the shade: for maximum intensity opt for large shades in pale colours.

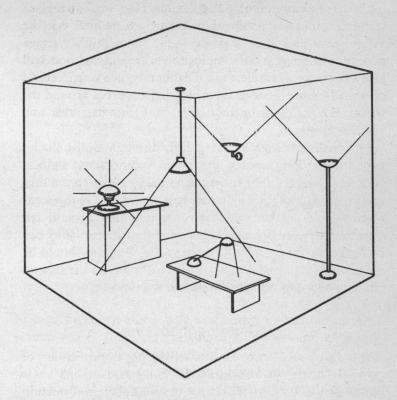

Distribute light from different sources around the room.

INDOOR ATMOSPHERE

A warm environment is a great comfort to most of us in winter, and especially to SAD sufferers. But finding the optimum balance between a comfortable indoor temperature and unhealthy and stuffy heat is not always easy. Studies carried out in working environments in England have found that temperatures above 23 degrees C (73 degrees F) produced sensations of stuffiness and discomfort. Yet many homes and offices are heated to this temperature or above.

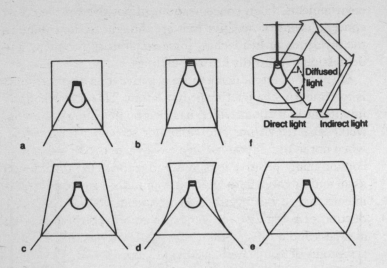

Lamp shades distribute light in different directions.

A comfortable temperature also needs a certain level of humidity (between thirty and sixty per cent). A dry atmosphere can be improved by distributing bowls of water around the house, and by having plenty of leafy plants; the transpiration through the leaves helps to regulate humidity and balance temperature.

Despite the need to keep the indoor environment warm, it is also essential to have a regular flow of fresh air through the building. Much illness and discomfort has been linked to the lack of negative ions present in indoor atmospheres. Ions are electrically charged molecules of air gases, some of which are negative, some positive. The negative ones are found in unpolluted areas and are thought to account for the beneficial feelings experienced after walking by the sea, near waterfalls or in open countryside. Positive ions on the other hand are produced by statically-charged surfaces, such as televisions, computers, synthetic materials and polluted, smoky environments. High concentrations of positive ions and low concentrations of negative ions are thought to contribute to the incidence of headaches, some respiratory problems and depression in centrally heated buildings.

One way of introducing more negative ions into the home is to regularly change the air in a room. This is particularly important in a room which has electric machinery running. Make sure televisions and computer screens are turned off when not in use. If you live in a city, where the air is likely to contain many positive ions, a negative ion generator known as an ionizer could help improve your indoor air. Some experiments carried out in office environments found that introduction of a negative ion generator improved the perceived alertness and atmospheric freshness of workers and reduced symptoms of headaches, nausea and dizziness.

Bringing plants and flowers into your home or workplace will also help to freshen the air. Plants absorb carbon dioxide in the air and produce oxygen, they also help restore the atmosphere with negative ions. Substitute chemical air fresheners with natural flowers, pot pourri or hanging dried flowers or herbs. Perfume the air with window boxes, holding fragrant flowers such as freesia or jasmine, taking care that they do not obscure the light.

FINDING A PERSONAL SPACE

Most people who suffer from SAD feel the need to get away from others and be alone at some time or other during the winter. For this reason it is important if you live with others to establish a personal space, nook or cranny, where you can go and not be disturbed. Ideally this would be a room where you could take refuge and implement all the suggestions outlined in this chapter, a sort of SAD haven, where you could sleep, read, write or pursue a hobby or interest in privacy.

Some people choose their personal space outside the house in a garage, workshop or greenhouse. If there is not a spare room available, you could corner off part of another room. I interviewed one woman who established her nook in the corner of a shared bedroom in a small apartment, where she set up a wicker screen and a sign saying 'thinking in progress, do not disturb!' Creating a personal space is part of your acceptance of SAD and your opportunity to nurture yourself through the winter.

17

Living With a SAD Sufferer

Living with someone who suffers from SAD can be a distressing and disturbing experience. It is always hard to watch loved ones suffer, and especially difficult to understand the sudden transformation SAD sufferers undergo from summer to winter. There is no doubt that the illness puts a burden on any relationship. Here are some examples of the feelings and reactions you may experience and the ways in which you can assist in making life more bearable for the sufferer and for yourself. In this chapter we will refer to the SAD sufferer as 'your friend', although he/she may, of course, be a partner or family member.

In a close relationship with someone who suffers SAD the first thing you will probably notice as winter approaches in that he/she seems to be irritable much of the time. Because this irritability is probably directed at you, it will be more obvious than other symptoms of SAD. Furthermore, it may generate differences of opinion and arguments. Another early sign is your friend's unwillingness to interact or socialize. He/she withdraws, spends time alone, falls asleep early in the evening, and shows no interest in physical contact. As winter draws on the other symptoms will appear in quick succession: your friend is unable to get out of bed, has no energy, feels helpless and inferior, is indecisive and avoids responsibility. Tension inevitably develops as you feel you are taking on more and more responsibility, but receiving no thanks, recognition or love in return. On the contrary, you are simply a buffer for your friend's misery and irritation.

Most people go through a bad patch from time to time; generally it is temporary and can be remedied by a little tender, loving care. However, in the case of SAD the symptoms get worse as winter progresses. As the months go by and tension builds up, you start to feel put upon, angry and hostile, instead of feeling pity and sympathy for your friend. Sarcastic comments, reproaches, judgements and criticism may be thrown about, which result in your friend withdrawing further, not only feeling exhausted and miserable, but guilty and inadequate to boot.

Of course this sequence of events need not happen if you are aware of what SAD is and how it affects your friend. That does not mean that you will never feel resentful, angry and hurt at times, as such a reaction would be abnormal. However, learning to channel these feelings will help you to cope with the illness, to give help to your friend and in general to allow your relationship to progress rather than decline.

The first rule to remember when feelings of anger and resentment arise is to direct them at the illness, not at the sufferer. The advantage of applying this rule is that your anger and frustration will be directed towards fighting the illness, not fighting your relationship.

Getting to know how SAD affects your friend and how he/she can be treated is the next step. A thorough read of this book will help to identify the symptoms your friend is experiencing, and to establish their severity. Knowledge of probable symptoms will help you to feel less frustrated and more understanding when confronted by them. Reading Chapter Four on SAD research, Chapter Six on SAD symptoms, and the self help SAD programme in Part Three will particularly help you to understand why the syndrome occurs, and how it can be treated. This will help you to support your friend in moves to combat SAD.

A correct diagnosis of SAD will explain why your friend is behaving as he/she is; it is then up to you to accept the autumn transition. Your position can only be one of acceptance: accepting that your friend is not the same person in winter as in summer; accepting that they cannot do as much; cannot react or think as quickly, cannot make decisions, cannot take responsibility; accepting that they may lose a job, or alienate friends; accepting that they may put on weight and, hardest of all, accepting that they may not appear to appreciate you, either emotionally or physically.

One of the most difficult things to accept for a person living with a SAD sufferer is the withdrawal of physical and emotional attachment. Loss of emotional expression is a common symptom for anyone who is depressed, and one which causes the most hurt and frustration to partners and families. It does not, however mean that your friend feels any less deeply for you; their feelings may be so bottled up that they are unable to express them, verbally or physically. Underneath the cold and wooden frontage, however, is a desperate need for your support and love, even if it cannot be returned immediately.

HOW CAN YOU HELP?

As a friend or relative of a SAD sufferer, you can be of enormous help if you can manage to establish a balance whereby you provide support, help and encouragement where necessary, while allowing your friend to maintain the independence and distance they need during the winter.

Treatment

You can help by encouraging your friend to have treatment. Visiting a doctor or clinic for diagnosis can require much courage and energy for a SAD sufferer, who may fear the consequences of being branded with a diagnosis of psychiatric illness. Encourage and accompany your friend if necessary. Take an interest in the treatment. Despite its tremendous therapeutic effect, phototherapy takes time and persistence. If your friend is feeling negative, he/she may give up and sink further into depression. You can help by participating in the treatment. Some couples keep the light box in the bedroom, and the non-SAD partner turns it on as soon as he/she awakens, to allow the other to surface gradually. Sitting with your friend, reading or playing a game while he/she is having therapy can make the process more bearable. The light box will not do you any harm, in fact you may get some benefit from it yourself.

If your friend is taking anti-depressant medication, have patience for the first few weeks of treatment while the drug takes its action. Although you may find it irritating having your nearest and dearest wandering around the house in pyjamas and acting like a zombie, don't forget that he/she is suffering too. Would you react so badly if he/she were laid up with appendicitis or a broken ankle?

Lifting Mood

When suffering from SAD your friend is likely to experience some of the symptoms of depression outlined in Chapters Six and Eleven. He/she will have a negative and distorted view of the world, and will interpret situations in a gloomy and hopeless way. You will probably not be able to radically change this attitude, but can help by gently proposing alternative, more positive angles. Be careful not to be drawn into an argument, however. Try to be encouraging rather than judgmental. Your friend's negativity will probably be so pervasive that he/she cannot see an end to the illness. You can reassure and remind him/her that the winter problems will pass.

Once therapy has relieved your friend's symptoms a little, then is the time to encourage him/her into a little more gentle activity. If there has been a break from work, try to ease him/her back. They may be unwilling to get out of the house and do things; however, activity will make them feel better, and is to be encouraged. Try to organize some gentle activities together that you will both enjoy; a regular common interest outside the home will divert you both from the problems of SAD.

Relieving the Burden

The most practical way to help SAD sufferers is to relieve them of some of the daily tasks which sap precious energy. Your friend may already be feeling too inadequate and guilty to ask you for more help, so it is best just to get on and do what you can, or arrange for someone else to help. Try to explain the illness to children, who may be puzzled by a parent's irritability, low energy levels and lack of affection. If they understand the situation, they will be more inclined to help. If you feel you are unable to cope, contact your doctor, who may be able to arrange for domestic help or child care.

Do not push important decisions onto your friend during the winter. He/she is probably lacking in confidence and feels indecisive. If possible, take responsibility for the payment of bills, and the management of monetary affairs. Your friend may be more forgetful or less conscientious during the winter. Take care, however, not to leave him/her feeling powerless, with nothing to do. As with everything, it is a question of striking a balance between doing too much and not doing enough.

Dealing with Threats of Suicide

Although there have been few reported incidents of suicide resulting from SAD, it is not entirely unheard of. A number of the sufferers I interviewed admitted that before discovering phototherapy they felt so desperate that suicide was a constant possibility. Threats of suicide can be extremely worrying and upsetting. Although it is commonly thought that people who threaten suicide rarely carry it through, this is not true, and therefore all suggestions should be taken seriously. If your friend makes any such reference it is time to consult the doctor. Take precautions not to leave medication or other potential toxins around the house. Try to keep a closer eye on your friend than normal to assess his/her mood. Try to share some of the distress by showing added love and affection.

Spring

The onset of spring is generally a time of great relief for SAD sufferers and their companions. However, sometimes the recovery is very rapid and is accompanied by an extreme swing in mood from depression to mania or hypomania, as described in Chapters Six and Fourteen. As winter draws to a close, SAD sufferers are often so pleased to be feeling better that they are unaware of the mood swing which takes them abnormally high and can result in strange behaviour, extreme overactivity and exhaustion. You can be of great help in these circumstances by watching out for sudden changes in mood and gently reminding your friend that he/she is becoming hypomanic. It may not be easy, as when in this state SAD sufferers are determined to make up for the time they have lost during the winter and it will be hard to keep up with them. If your friend's behaviour seems seriously abnormal, or if their actions have serious consequences on your daily life or relationship, do not hesitate to consult your doctor or psychiatrist. It may be that your friend requires medication which will help to combat the destructive and sometimes dangerous mood swing which occurs in spring. Chapter Fourteen outlines how to recognize hypomania or mania and suggests ways of coping with it.

If you are married to or cohabiting with a SAD sufferer you

may find the sudden swing in mood in spring time brings a renewed interest in sex. For some, this is a welcome change after a winter of celibacy. For others, the rapid increase in sexual energy of a SAD partner can be disconcerting. After months of rejection and frustration you may resent the sexual demands which are suddenly made. You may find that the relationship has changed in physical and emotional ways and cannot continue as it was before. The break up of partnerships under the strain of SAD is not uncommon. Talking over problems together or with a doctor or counsellor can sometimes help to breach the gap which forms over the winter months. Some couples find that the struggle to fight SAD pulls them together, and they learn to live with the annual lulls and peaks of mood, energy and sexual activity, enduring the bad times and making the most of the good.

While you may want to do as much as possible for your partner or friend, your relationship will have more chance of survival if you manage to maintain a certain independence. Do not give up your job or interests outside the home; get out and see people even if your friend prefers to stay at home. The benefits of having a change of scenery and company are many: it gives you a well-deserved break, from which you will return refreshed, and it allows your friend the space and independence he/she requires during the winter. Moreover, the less your life is disrupted the less you will resent your friend or the illness and the less reason he/she will have to feel guilty.

Do not resist the opportunity to talk to others occasionally about your problems. If you cannot confide in a friend, try joining a self help organization (see Resources section) where you can talk to others with similar experiences and problems, as this can bring great relief and support. Your friend should also be encouraged to join the group and communicate with other SAD sufferers if possible. The opportunity to share thoughts and feelings with others who have been through a similar experience is very valuable. Above all, it will allow you to protect yourself from being pulled down into the abyss of depression, which so often happens to those living with or caring for depressed friends or relatives. Despite all the difficulties and sorrow winter may bring, if you can maintain your sparkle and enthusiasm for life, you are much more likely to pass it on to others.

Resources

SAD RESEARCH CENTRES AND CLINICS

Australia

Stuart Armstrong Ph.D.
Department of Psychology
La Trobe University
Bundoora
Victoria 3083

Dr Philip Boyce
Department of Psychiatry
Nepean Hospital
P.O. Box 63
Penrith
N.S. Wales 2750

Dr Peter Marriott
Suite 1, 140 Church St
Richmond
Victoria 3121

Austria

Siegfried Kasper, MD
Department of Psychiatry
University of Vienna
Allgemeines Krankenhous der
  Stadt Wien
Wahringer Gurtel 18–20
A–1010 Wein

Josef Schwitzer, MD
Christian Neudorfer, MD
Univ. Klinik fur Psychiatrie
Anichstrasse 35
A–6020 Innsbruck

Canada

Carl Blashko, MD
Cedars Professional Park
2923 66th Street
Edmonton, Alberta T62 4C1

Gail Eskes, Ph.D.
Department of Psychology
Dalhousie University
Halifax, Nova Scotia B3H 4J1

A-Missagh Ghadirian, MD
Seasonal Affective Disorders/
  Mood Disorders Clinic
McGill University
Royal Victorian Hospital
1025 Pine Avenue West
Montreal, Quebec H3A 1A1

Chris Gorman, MD
704 3031 Hospital Drive,
  N.W.
Calgary, Alberta T2N 2T8

Edward Horn, MD
Royal Ottawa Hospital
1145 Carling Avenue
Ottawa, Ontario K1Z 7K4

Raymond Lam MD
Department of Psychiatry
University of British Columbia
2255 Westbrook Mall
Vancouver BC V6T 2A1

Anthony Levitt, MD
Clarke Institute of Psychiatry
250 College Street
Toronto, Ontario M5T 1R8

Charles Mate-Kole, Ph.D.
Nova Scotia Rehab Centre
Dalhousie University
1341 Hill Hospital
Abbie J. Lane Building
1763 Robie Street
Halifax, Nova Scotia
B3H 3G2

Harvey Moldofsky, MD
Centre for Sleep and
  Chronobiology
University of Toronto
The Toronto Hospital,
  Western Division
399 Bathurst Street
Toronto, Ontario M5T 2S8

Rachel Morehouse, MD
Sleep Disorders Laboratory
Dalhousie University
Room 4008, Abbie J. Lane
  Building
1763 Robie Street
Halifax, Nova Scotia
B3H 3G2

Colin M. Shapiro, Ph.D.
Department of Psychiatry
The Toronto Hospital,
  Western Division
399 Bathurst Street
Toronto, Ontario M5T 2S8

Meir Steiner, MD
Department of Psychiatry and
  Biomedical Sciences
McMaster University
Hamilton, Ontario

Finland

Carl Hagfors, Ph.D.
Department of Psychology
University of Jyvaskyla
P.O. Box 35
40351 Jyvaskyla

Timo Partonen MD
Ilomaentie 11 B 36
00840 Helsinki 84

France

Dr Yves Prigent
Hôtel Dieu – Centre
    Hospitalier
B.P. 67
F–29120 Pont-L'Abbé

Dan Waniek, MD
Laboratory of Biochemistry
Hopital Pitie-Salpetriere
War, Inc. Eye Image Analysis
93400 Saint Ouen

Germany

Henner Giedke MD
Osianderstr 22
D–72076 Tübingen

Wilfried Kohler, Ph.D.
Heinrich-Hofman Strasse 10
D–6000 Frankfort am Main

Dr Eckart Ruther
Psychiatr. Klinik d. Universität
V. Sieboldstr. 5
D–37075 Göttingen

Iceland

Andres Magnusson, MD
Department of Psychiatry
National University Hospitals
Box 10
121 Reykjavik

Ireland

Philip Carney, MD
Department of Psychiatry
University College Hospital
Galway

Italy

Guiseppe Barbato, MD
Sezione di Psichiatria
Universita Degli Studi di
    Napoli Federico II
Via Sergio Pansini, 5
80131 Napoli

Alessandro Meluzzi, MD
Unita Sanitaria Local Regione
    Piemonte
Clinical Psychiatric University
    of Torino
10126 Torino

Giovanni Muscettola, MD
Department of Psychiatry
Medical School
University of Trieste
Via S. Cilino 16 Trieste

Japan

Tatsuro Ohta, MD
Department of Psychiatry
Nagoya University School of
    Medicine
65 Tsurumai-cho, Showa-ku
Nagoya 466

Kiyohisa Takahashi, MD
National Institute of
    Neuroscience NCNP
4–1–1, Ogawahigashi, Kodaira
Tokyo 187

The Netherlands

Dr D Beersma, Dr M Gordijn,
Dr Y Meesters, Dr R van den
Hoofdakker
Department of Biological
    Psychiatry
University of Groningen
Oostersingel 59
9713 EZ Groningen

Norway

Odd Lingjaerde, MD
Gaustad Sykehus
Boks 24, Gaustad
N–0320 Oslo 3

Trond Bratlid, MD
Asgard Hospital
N–9000 Tromso

Sweden

Dr Roger Wibom
N.I.O.H.
Division of Neuromedicine
    IMN
S–17184 Solna

Torbjorn Akerstedt, Ph.D.
Karolinska Institute
Box 60205
S. 10401 Stockholm

Johan Beck-Friis, MD
Department of Psychiatry
Karolinska Institute
Saint Gorans Hospital
S–11281 Stockholm

Bengt Kjellman, MD
Department of Psychiatry
Karolinska Institute
Saint Forans Hospital
S–11281 Stockholm

Bjorn-Erik Thalen, MD
Karolinska Institute
Box 12500
S–11281 Stockholm

Switzerland

Anna Wirz-Justice, Ph.D.
Psychiatrische
    Universitätsklinik Basel
Wilhelm Klein-Strasse 27
CH–4025 Basel

UK

Professor Chris Thompson MD
Department of Psychiatry
Royal South Hants Hospital
Graham Road
Southampton SO9 4PE

Stuart Checkley MD
Maudsley Hospital
De Crespigny Park
London SE5 8AF

Dr Robert Tresman
Mental Health Unit
Lister Hospital
Coreys Mill Lane
Stevenage SG1 4AB

Dr G Vincenti
Department of Mental Health
Friarage Hospital
Northallerton
N. Yorks DL6 1JG

Dr John Eagles
Ross Clinic
Royal Cornhill Hospital
Cornhill Road
Aberdeen AB9 2ZF

USA

CALIFORNIA
Chris Gillin MD,
Barbara Parry MD
Department of Psychiatry
UCSD
La Jolla CA 92093

Daniel Kripke MD
Circadian Pacemaker
  Laboratory
9500 Gilman Drive
La Jolla CA 92093

David Sack MD
3340 Los Coyotes Diagonal
Long Beach CA 90908

FLORIDA
Robert Skwerer MD
5600 Bee Ridge Rd, Suite B
Sarasota FL 34233

ILLINOIS
Charmane Eastman Ph.D.
Biological Rhythms Research
  Laboratory
Rush Presbyterian-St Luke's
  Medical Center
1653 West Congress Parkway
Chicago IL 60612

MARYLAND
Affective Disorders Clinic
Johns Hopkins University
  School of Medicine
Meyer 3–181
Baltimore MD 21287

Dr Normal Rosenthal,
Dr Thomas Wehr
National Institute of Mental
  Health
Bldg 10, Room 4S–239
9000 Rockville Pike
Bethesda MD 20892

MASSACHUSETTS
Martin Teicher MD
McLean Hospital
115 Mill St
Belmont MA 02178

Janis Anderson Ph.D.
SAD Clinic
Brigham and Women's
  Hospital
221 Longwood Ave
Boston MA 02115

MICHIGAN
Oliver Cameron MD
University of Michigan
Riverview Building
900 Wall St J232
Ann Arbor MI 48109

MINNESOTA
Paul Arbisi Ph.D.
Minneapolis Veterans
  Medical Center
One Veterans Drive
Minneapolis MN 55417

NEW YORK
Michael Terman Ph.D.
New York State Psychiatric
  Institute
722 West 168th St, Box 50
New York NY 10032

Richard Kavey MD
2922 Eager Rd
Lafayette NY 13084

OREGON
Alfred Lewy MD, Robert
  Sack MD
Department of Psychiatry
University of Oregon Health
  Sciences Center

3181 SW Sam Jackson Park
  Rd
Portland OR 97401

PENNSYLVANIA
George Brainard Ph.D.
Department of Neurology
Jefferson Medical College
1025 Walnut St
Philadelphia PA 19107

Michael Thase Ph.D.
University of Pittsburgh
  School of Medicine
3811 O'Hara St
Pittsburgh PA 15241

RHODE ISLAND
Mark Bauer MD
Department of Psychiatry
Brwon University
Providence RI 02912

WASHINGTON
David Avery MD
Harborview Medical Center
325 9th Ave
Seattle WA 98104

SUPPORT GROUPS

UK

SAD Association (SADA)
P.O. Box 989
London SW7 2PZ

The SAD Association is a voluntary organization and registered charity which informs the public and health professions about SAD and supports and advises sufferers of the illness. SADA produces a newsletter three times a year and other publications, holds meetings, has a network of contacts and local groups, a lightbox hire scheme, and raises money for research into SAD.

For free basic information about SAD and its treatments, send an s.a.e. to SADA at the above address. For full details of SAD treatments, how to hire, buy and use light fixtures, list of contacts, telephone helpline, local groups, meetings, books, research updates and GP information, please send £5 (£3 concessions) to the above address.

USA

NOSAD
P.O. Box 40133
Washington DC 20016

NOSAD operates in much the same way as SADA, providing information about SAD by means of an information package and newsletters, and offering support to sufferers and their families and friends.

New Zealand

SAD Society
P.O. Box 314
Waiuku

FURTHER SOURCES OF INFORMATION

USA

Society for Light Treatment and Biological Rhythms (SLTBR)
10200 West 44 St, Suite 304
Wheat Ridge, CO 80033

Seasonal Studies Program
National Institute of Mental Health
Building 10, Room 4S–239
9000 Rockville Pike
Bethesda, MD 20892

WHERE TO PURCHASE LIGHT FIXTURES

Finland

Auradent
Puutarhakatu 12
20100 Turku
Tel (021) 233 1155
Fax (021) 233 1148

France

Durolux
22 Rue Madiraa
92400 Courbevoie
Tel (1) 47 68 90 80
Fax (1) 43 33 41 21

Germany

SML Licht u.
   Bestrahlungssysteme
Schleidener Strasse 136
D-5100 Aachen
Tel (02408) 80527
Fax (02408) 80851

Italy

Natura-Lite s.r.l.
Via Luigi Kossuth 36
00149 Rome
Tel (06) 526 2048
Fax (06) 526 2248

Norway

Miljo LYS A/S
Bromsvn. 9
3183 Horten
Tel (0330) 44912
Fax (0330) 47245

Sweden

Ratt Ljus AB
Osmundsvagen 37
Box 11159, 161 11 Bromma
Tel (08) 250806
Fax (08) 800665

Switzerland

Elec Handels AG
Eichenweg 33
CH-8121 Benglen
Tel (01) 825 2414
Fax (01) 825 2873

UK

FSL/The SAD Lightbox Co Ltd
Unit 1, Riverside Business
   Centre
Victoria Street
High Wycombe, Bucks
   HP11 2LT
Tel (01494) 526051/448727
Fax (01494) 527005

Arthur McKay & Co. Ltd.
7/9 Arthur Street
Edinburgh EH6 5DA
Tel (0131) 554 0611

Outside In (Cambridge) Ltd
Unit 3, Scotland Road Estate
Dry Drayton
Cambridge CB3 8AT
Tel (01954) 211955
Fax (01954) 211966
Internet connection:
   http://www.outsidein.co.uk

Sunbox Designs Ltd
43 Woodberry Crescent
Muswell Hill
London N10 1PJ
Tel (0181) 444 9201/9218

Viewboxes Ltd
Freepost MK1241
Granby
Milton Keynes MK1 1XA
(01908) 642323

USA

The Sunbox Company
19217 Orbit Drive
Gaithersburg, MD 20879
Tel (301) 869 5980

Medie-Light, Inc
Yacht Club Drive
Lake Hopatcong, NJ 07849
Tel (201) 663 1214

Apollo Light Systems, Inc
352 West 1060 South
Orem UT 84058
Tel (800) 545 9667

Bibliography

This is not a complete bibliography but a selected collection of publications for further reference.

General Reading

Rosenthal, N., Blehar, M. (eds), (1989), *Seasonal Affective Disorders and Phototherapy* (Guilford Press, New York).

Rosenthal, N. (1989), *Seasons of the Mind* (Bantam Books, New York).

Thompson, C., Silverstone, T. (eds), (1990), *Seasonal Affective Disorders* (CNS Neuroscience Press, London).

Chapter 1

Boyce, P., Parker, G. (1988), 'Seasonal Affective Disorder in the Southern Hemisphere', *American Journal of Psychiatry* vol. 145:1, pp. 96–9.

Jones W.H.S (ed), Withington E.T. (trans) (1923–31), *Works of Hippocrates* Volumes 1–4 (Harvard University Press, Cambridge, MA, USA).

Garvey, M. Wesner, R. Godes, M. (1988), 'Comparison of Seasonal and Nonseasonal Affective Disorders', *American Journal of Psychiatry* vol. 145:1, pp. 100–102.

Kasper, S., Wehr, T., Bartko, J., Gaist, P., Rosenthal, N. (1988), 'Epidemiological Findings of Seasonal Changes in

Mood and Behavior', *Archives of General Psychiatry*, vol. 46, pp. 823–33.

McIntyre, I., Armstrong, S., Norman, T. (1989), 'Treatment of Seasonal Affective Disorder with Light: Preliminary Australian Experience', *Australian and New Zealand Journal of Psychiatry* vol. 23, pp. 369–72.

Rosenthal, N., *et al.* (1985), 'Antidepressant Effects of Light in Seasonal Affective Disorder', *American Journal of Psychiatry*, vol. 142:2, pp. 163–70.

Sonis, W. (1990), 'Seasonal Affective Disorder of Childhood and Adolescence: A Review', in N. Rosenthal, and M. Blehar (eds), *Seasonal Affective Disorder and Phototherapy* (Guilford Press, New York).

Terman, M. *et al.* (1990). 'Seasonal Symptom Patterns in New York: Patients and Population', in C. Thompson and T. Silverstone (eds), *Seasonal Affective Disorders* (CNS Neuroscience Press, London).

Thompson, C., Isaacs, G. (1988), 'Seasonal Affective Disorder – a British Sample, Symptomatology in relation to mode of referral and diagnostic subtype', *Journal of Affective Disorders*, vol. 14, pp. 1–11.

Wehr, T., Sack, A., Rosenthal, N. (1987), 'Seasonal Affective Disorder With Summer Depression and Winter Hypomania', *American Journal of Psychiatry*, vol. 144:12, pp. 1602–03.

Wirz-Justice, A., *et al.* (1986), 'Light Treatment of Seasonal Affective Disorder in Switzerland', *Acta Psychiatrica Scandinavia*, vol. 74, pp. 193–204.

Chapter 2

Aschoff, J. (1981), 'Annual Rhythms in Man', in J. Aschoff, *Biological Rhythms, Handbook of Behavioural Neurobiology*, vol. 4 (Plenum Publishing Corp. New York).

Grahame K., (1908), *The Wind in the Willows* (Methuen London).

Gwinner, E. (1981), 'Annual Rhythms: Perspective, and Circannual Systems', in J. Aschoff (ed), *Biological Rhythms, Handbook of Behavioural Neurobiology,* vol. 4 (Plenum Publishing Corp., New York).

Wehr, T., Goodwin, F. (1983), *Circadian Rhythms in Psychiatry* (The Boxwood Press).

Chapter 3

Isaacs, G., Stainer, T., Sensky, T., Moor, S., Thompson, C., (1988), 'Phototherapy and its mechanism of action in seasonal affective disorder', *Journal of Affective Disorders,* vol. 14, pp. 13–19.

Lewy, A., Kern, H., Rosenthal, N., Wehr, T. (1982), 'Bright Artificial Light treatment of a manic-depressive patient with a seasonal mood cycle', *American Journal of Psychiatry,* vol. 139, pp. 1496–1498.

Lewy, A., Sack, R., Singer, C., White, D. (1987), 'Antidepressant and circadian phase-shifting effects of light', *Science,* vol. 235, pp. 352–354.

Lewy, A., Sack, R., Singer, C., White, D. (1987), 'The phase shift hypothesis for bright light's therapeutic mechanism of action: theoretical considerations and experimental evidence', *Psychopharmacology Bulletin,* vol. 23, pp. 349–353.

Murphy, D., Aba, B., Winton, F., *et al.* (1990), 'Seasonal affective disorder: a neurophysiological approach', in C. Thompson and T. Silverstone (eds), *Seasonal Affective Disorders* (CNS Neuroscience, London).

Rosenthal, N., Jacobson, M., Sack, D., Arendt, J., *et al.* (1988), 'Atenolol in Seasonal Affective Disorder: a test of melatonin hypothesis', *American Journal of Psychiatry,* vol. 145:1, pp. 52–6.

Rosenthal, N. (1990), 'New Concept and Developments in Seasonal Affective Disorder' in C. Thompson and T. Silverstone (eds), *Seasonal Affective Disorders*, (CNS Neuroscience Press, London).

Thompson, C., Isaacs, G. (1988), 'Seasonal affective disorder – a British sample: Symptomatology in relation to mode of referral and diagnostic subtype', *Journal of Affective Disorder*, vol. 14, pp. 1–11.

Silverstone, T. (1990), 'The clinical psychopharmacology of seasonal affective disorder', in C. Thompson and T. Silverstone (eds), *Seasonal Affective Disorders* (CNS Neuroscience, London).

Terman, M. (1988), 'On the question of mechanism in phototherapy for seasonal affective disorder: considerations of clinical efficacy and epidemiology', *Journal of Biological Rhythms*, vol. 3., no. 2, pp. 155–172.

Terman, M., Terman, J., (1990), 'New light on winter depression', *Clinical Advances in the Treatment of Psychiatric Disorders*, vol 4:1, pp. 1–11.

Winton, F., Corn, T., Huson, W., Franey, C., Arendt, J., and Checkley, S. (1989), 'Effects of light treatment upon mood and melatonin in patients with seasonal affective disorder', *Psychological Medicine*, vol. 19, pp. 585–590.

Wirz-Justice, A., Graw, P., Buchelli, C., *et al.* (1986), 'Seasonal affective disorder in Switzerland: a clinical perspective', in C. Thompson and T. Silverstone (eds), *Seasonal Affective Disorders* (CNS Neuroscience Press, London).

Chapter 4

Laszlo, J., (1969), 'Observations on two new artificial lights for reptile displays', *International Zpp Yearbook*, vol. 9, pp. 12–13.

Maas, J., Jayson, J., Kleiber, D. (1974), 'Effects of spectral differences in illumination on fatigue', *Journal of Applied Psychology*, vol. 59, no. 4, pp. 524–526.

Okudaira, N., Kripke, D., Webster, J. (1983), 'Naturalistic studies of human light exposure', *American Journal of Physiology*, vol. 25, pp. R613–15.

Ott, J., (1973), *Health and Light: the effects of natural and artificial light on man and other living things* (Pocket Books, New York).

Chapter 5

Downes, A., Blunt, T. (1877), 'Researches on the Effect of Light upon Bacteria and Other Organisms', *Proceedings of the Royal Society of Medicine*, vol. 26, 488.

Kasper, S., *et al.* (1989), 'Phototherapy in Individuals With and Without Sub-syndromal Seasonal Affective Disorder', *Archives of General Psychiatry*, vol. 46, pp. 837–844.

Kripke, D., *et al.* (1989), 'Phototherapy for Nonseasonal Major Depressive Disorders' in N. Rosenthal and M. Blehar (eds), *Seasonal Affective Disorders and Phototherapy*, (Guilford Press, New York).

Lewy, A., Wehr, T., Goodwin, F., Newsome, S., Markey, S. (1980), 'Light suppresses melatonin secretion in humans', *Science*, vol. 210, 1267.

McIntyre, I. (1990), 'A portable light source for bright light treatment', *Sleep*, vol. 13, pp. 277–80 (Raven Press, New York).

Parry, B., *et al.* (1989), 'Morning versus evening bright light treatment of late luteal phase dysphoric disorder', *American Journal of Psychiatry*, vol. 146:9, pp. 1215–17.

Posers, L., Terman, M., Link, M. (1989), 'Bright light treatment of night-shift workers', Abstract of paper presented at Society for Light Treatment and Biological Rhythms, National Institute of Health, Bethesda, MD.

Rosenthal, N., *et al.* (1984), 'Seasonal affective disorder, a description of the syndrome and preliminary findings with light therapy', *Archives of General Psychiatry*, vol. 41, pp. 72–80.

Sasaki, M., Kuorsaki, Y., 'Effects of bright light on circadian rhythmicity and sleep after transmeridian flight,' and Cole, R., Kripke, D., 'Amelioration of Jet Lag by Bright Light Treatment effects of sleep consolidation' (1989), in *Sleep Research*, Vol. 18 (Brain Information Service/Brain Research Institute, UCLA).

Sonis, W. (1989), 'Seasonal Affective Disorder of Childhood and Adolescence: A review', in N. Rosenthal and M. Blehar (eds), *Seasonal Affective Disorders and Phototherapy* (Guilford Press, New York).

Stinson, D., Thompson, C. (1990), 'Clinical Experience with Phototherapy', *Journal of Effective Disorders*, vol. 18, pp. 129–135

Terman, M., and Terman, J. (1990), 'New Light on Winter Depression', *Clinical Advances in the Treatment of Psychiatric Disorders*, vol. 4:1, pp. 1–11.

Terman, M., *et al.* (1990), 'Bright Light Therapy for Winter Depression: Potential Ocular Effects and Theoretical Implications', *Photochemistry and Photobiology*, vol. 51.

Chapter 6

Depression

Beck, A., (1984), 'Antidote to Depression', in *Psychology Today* (American Psychological Association, Washington DC).

Beck, A., Emery, G. (1985), *Anxiety Disorders and Phobias* (Basic Books, Inc, New York).

Eating and appetite

Kruachi, K., Wirz-Justice, A. (1988), 'The Four Seasons: Food Intake Frequency in Seasonal Affective Disorder in the Course of a Year', *Psychiatry Research*, vol. 25, pp. 323–338.

Kruachi, K., Wirz-Justice, A., Graw, P. (in press), 'The Relationship of Affective State to Dietary Preference: Winter Depression and Light therapy as a Model', *Journal of Affective Disorders*.

O'Rourke, D., *et al.* (1989), 'Treatment of Seasonal Depression with d-Fenfluramine', *Journal of Clinical Psychiatry*, vol. 50:9, pp. 343–347.

Rosenthal, N. *et al.* (1989) 'Seasonal Affective Disorder: Relevance for the Treatment and Research of Bulimia' in Hudson, J. and Pope, H. (eds), *Psychobiology of Bulimia* (American Psychiatric Press).

Rosenthal, N., *et al.* (1989), 'Psychobiological Effects of Carbohydrate- and Protein-Rich Meals in Patients with Seasonal Affective Disorder and Normal Controls', *Biological Psychiatry*, vol. 25, pp. 1029–40.

Wurtman, R., Wurtman, J. (1984), 'Nutrients, Neurotransmitter Synthesis, and the control of food intake' in A. Sunkard and E. Stellar (eds), *Eating and Its Disorders* (Raven Press, New York).

Sleep

The American Medical Association, *Straight-talk, No-nonsense Guide to Better Sleep* (1984) (Random House, New York).

Langen, D. (1978), *Speaking of Sleeping Problems: Learning to Sleep Well Again* (Consolidated Book Publishers, New York).

Skwerer, R., *et al.* (1989), 'Neurobiology of Seasonal Affective Disorder and Phototherapy', in N. Rosenthal and M. Blehar (eds) *Seasonal Affective Disorders and Phototherapy* (Guilford Press, New York).

Mania

Carney, P., Fitzgerald C., Monaghan, C. (1990), 'Seasonal Variations in Mania' in C. Thompson and T. Silverstone (eds), *Seasonal Affective Disorders* (CNS Neuroscience Press, London).

Dewhurst, K. (1962), 'A Seventeenth-Century Symposium on Manic Depressive Psychosis', *British Journal of Medical Psychology*, vol. 35, pp. 769–771.

Jones, W.H.S., Withington, E.T., (trans), (1923–31), Works of Hippocrates, volumes 1–4 (Harvard University Press, Cambridge, MA, USA).

Kraepelin, E. (1921), 'Manic Depressive Insanity and Paranoia', G. Robertson (ed), R. Barclay (trans) (E. & S. Livingstone, Edinburgh).

Rosenthal, N. *et al.* (1983), 'Seasonal Cycling in a Bipolar Patient', *Psychiatry Research* vol. 8, pp. 25–31.

Thompson, C., *et al.* (1988), 'A Comparison of Normal, Bipolar and Seasonal Affective Disorder Subjects Using the Seasonal Pattern Assessment Questionnaire', *Journal of Affective Disorders*, vol. 14, pp. 257–264.

Wehr, T. (1989), 'Seasonal Affective Disorders: A Historical Overview', in N. Rosenthal and M. Blehar (eds), *Seasonal Affective Disorders and Phototherapy*. (Guilford Press, New York).

Chapter 8

Isaacs, G., Stainer, D., Sensky, T., Moor, S., Thompson, C. (1988), 'Phototherapy and its mechanism of action in seasonal affective disorder', *Journal of Affective Disorders*, vol. 14, pp. 13–19.

Rosenthal, N., Skwerer, R., Jacobsen, F., Hardin, T., Wehr, T., 'Phototherapy: The NIMH Experience', in C. Thompson and T. Silverstone (eds) *Seasonal Affective Disorders* (1990), (CNS Neuroscience Press, London).

Terman, M., Reme, C., Rafferty, B., Gallin, P., Terman, J. (1990), 'Bright Light Therapy for Winter Depression: Potential Ocular Effects and Theoretical Implications', *Photochemistry and Photobiology*, vol. 51.

Terman, M. 'Light Therapy' in M. Kryger, T. Roth and W. Dement (eds) (1989), *Principles and Practice of Sleep Medicine* (W.B. Saunders Company, Philadelphia).

Chapter 9

Manic Depression Fellowship, *Drug Treatment of Manic Depression*.

Kuipers, L., Bebbington, P. (1987), *Living with Mental Illness, A book for relatives and friends,* (Souvenir Press, London).

Chapter 10

Kuipers, L., Bebbington, P. (1987), *Living with Mental Illness, A book for relatives and friends*, (Souvenir Press, London).

Chapter 11

Beck, A. (1967), *Depression causes and treatment* (University of Pennsylvania Press, Philadelphia).

Burns, D., (1980), *Feeling Good The New Mood Therapy* (William Morrow & Co Inc, New York).

Chapter 12

Lieberman, H., Wurtman, J., Chew, B. (1986), 'Changes in mood after carbohydrate consumption among obese individuals', *American Journal of Clinical Nutrition,* vol. 44, pp. 772–8.

Rosenthal, N., *et al.* (1989), 'Psychobiological effects of carbohydrate- and protein-rich meals in patients with seasonal affective disorder and normal controls', *Biological Psychiatry*, vol. 23, pp. 1029–40.

Wurtman, R., Wurtman, J. (January 1989), 'Carbohydrates and Depression', *Scientific American*, pp. 50–57.

Kruachi, K., Wirz-Justice, A., Graw, P., 'The relationship of affective state to dietary preference: winter depression and light therapy as a model' (personal communication).

Chapter 13

The American Medical Association, *Straight-talk, No-nonsense Guide to Better Sleep* (Random House, New York).

Langen, D. (1978), *Speaking of Sleeping Problems: Learning to Sleep Well Again* (Consolidated Book Publishers).

Chapter 15

McCann, L., Holmes, D. (1984), 'Influence of aerobic exercise on depression', *Journal of Personality and Social Psychology*, vol. 46:5, pp. 1142–47.

Kenton, L. (1983), *The Joy of Beauty* (Century Publishing, London).

Davis, F., (1980), *Living Alive* (Doubleday & Company, Inc., New York).

Chapter 17

Eastwood, J., (1987–1990), SADAssociation newsletters (SADAssociation, London).

Kuipers, L., Bebbington, P. (1987), *Living with Mental Illness, A book for relatives and friends* (Souvenir Press, London).

Sturgeon, W. (1970), *Depression How to recognise it, how to treat it, and how to grow from it* (Prentice Hall, London).

Index

Of further interest . . .

MELATONIN

Hasnain Walji, PhD

If you were offered a non-prescription pill containing a naturally occurring substance that induces sleep, banishes jet lag and has anti-ageing properties, would you believe it to be true?

Now a pill containing this substance is available – a hormone called melatonin. The functions of melatonin were until recently a mystery. Now it is believed that this hormone secreted by the pineal gland may have a major impact in the management of sleep disorders, jet lag and even the ageing process itself. Hasnain Walji, PhD, looks at the latest research into melatonin, exploring its potential, and advises who will obtain most benefit from the supplement and how it should be used.

ENERGIZE YOURSELF

*A complete guide to restoring
lost vitality and strength*

Vera Peiffer

This practical handbook not only looks at the causes of depleted energy, but also suggests ways in which you can recharge your physical and emotional batteries. Vera Peiffer introduces many down-to-earth methods and techniques aimed at achieving this, all of which are highly effective and fun to carry out.

Discover the benefits of vitamins and minerals, detoxifying, rebounding, breathing, stretching, relaxing, meditating, creative visualization, enjoying music, homoeopathy, shiatsu and much, much more.

Ideal for anyone who feels lethargic, listless or who has recently been ill, *Energize Yourself* is essential reading for anyone needing a kick start in life.

HEALING THROUGH NUTRITION

A natural approach to treating
50 common illnesses with diet and nutrients

Dr Melvyn R. Werbach

This indispensable reference book provides the nutritional roots of and treatments for 50 common illnesses, from allergies and the common cold to cancer.

The world's authority on the relationship between nutrition and illness, Dr Melvyn Werbach makes it easy to learn what you can do to influence the course of your health via the nutrients that you feed your body. A chapter is devoted to each of the 50 ailments and this highly accessible A–Z of nutritional health includes:

- an analysis of dietary factors affecting health and well-being
- a suggested healing diet for 50 common illnesses
- nutritional healing plans, with recommended dosages for vitamins, minerals and other essential nutrients
- an explanation of vitamin supplements and how they can improve your health

There are also guidelines on how to plan the right healing diet for yourself and how to diagnose food sensitivities. With this groundbreaking guide you will be able to make informed decisions about the essential role of nutrients in your health and well-being.

LET'S EAT RIGHT TO KEEP FIT

Adelle Davis

Here Adelle Davis presents information concerning our bodies' vital nutritional processes which is both authoritative and fascinating. Her recommendations for a balanced diet are important for anyone interested in preventive medicine.

Over 40 nutrients needed by the body for health are discussed in detail and the foods that supply them are listed.

Described by *Time* magazine as 'the highest authority in the kitchen', the value of good wholesome food over synthetic foods is stressed throughout. This book remains a bible for anyone interested in health or food – from doctors to cooks.

5494

LET'S GET WELL

Adelle Davis

Let's Get Well explains how a well chosen diet, which provides the most needed nutrients, can repair and rebuild a sick body. Packed full of information on every aspect of health and nutrition, it is an ideal reference book for the way we live today.

Adelle Davis explains the function of nutrition in diseases related to the blood system, the digestion, the liver, the kidneys and the nervous system. Illnesses covered include heart attacks, ulcers, diabetes, arthritis, gout and anaemia. Her clear explanations, with full medical references, will guide the way to better health.

MELATONIN	0 7225 3225 3	£3.99	☐
ENERGIZE YOURSELF	0 7225 3111 7	£6.99	☐
HEALING THROUGH NUTRITION	0 7225 2941 4	£16.99	☐
BOOK OF PAIN RELIEF	0 7225 2820 5	£7.99	☐
LET'S EAT RIGHT TO KEEP FIT	0 7225 3203 2	£5.99	☐
LET'S GET WELL	0 7225 2701 2	£5.99	☐
HEALTHY BY NATURE	0 7225 2803 5	£9.99	☐

All these books are available from your local bookseller or can be ordered direct from the publishers.

To order direct just tick the titles you want and fill in the form below:

Name: _____

Address: _____

_____

_____ Postcode: _____

Send to: Thorsons Mail Order, Dept 3, HarperCollins*Publishers*, Westerhill Road, Bishopbriggs, Glasgow G64 2QT.
Please enclose a cheque or postal order or your authority to debit your Visa/Access account –

Credit card no: _____

Expiry date: _____

Signature: _____

– to the value of the cover price plus:
UK & BFPO: Add £1.00 for the first book and 25p for each additional book ordered.
Overseas orders including Eire: Please add £2.95 service charge. Books will be sent by surface mail but quotes for airmail despatches will be given on request.

24 HOUR TELEPHONE ORDERING SERVICE FOR ACCESS/VISA CARDHOLDERS – TEL: 0141 772 2281.